CB129993

Personal Best

Workbook

B1
Pre-intermediate

Series Editor
Jim Scrivener

Authors
Elizabeth Walter
and **Kate Woodford**

Richmond

UNIT 1

All about me

1A LANGUAGE

GRAMMAR: Simple present and adverbs of frequency

1 Order the words to complete the sentences.

1 gets together with / her friend Pat / sometimes
Gloria ________________ for coffee.
2 hardly ever / the bus / takes
Daniel ________________ to work.
3 ride your bike / you / often
Do ________________ to the office?
4 never / any / does
Miguel ________________ housework.
5 listen / to / often
We ________________ the radio.
6 visit / always / my friend
I ________________ on the weekend.
7 see / she / does / often
How ________________ Mario?
8 study / usually / don't
They ________________ in the morning.
9 to / sometimes / goes
Silvia ________________ the theater.
10 usually / eat / doesn't
Alicia ________________ breakfast.

2 Complete the sentences with the correct form of the verbs in parentheses.

1 Greta ____________ two brothers. (have)
2 Peter ____________ his hair every day. (wash)
3 My friend Enrique ____________ in a factory. (work)
4 Marta and Luis ____________ in Buenos Aires; they live in Brasília. (not live)
5 ____________ you ____________ Portuguese? (speak)
6 Ben ____________ to Europe every summer to visit his family. (fly)
7 We ____________ swimming. (not like)
8 ____________ they ____________ to the same school as you? (go)

VOCABULARY: Personality adjectives

3 Match descriptions 1–8 with adjectives a–h.

1 Anna often says things that upset other people. ____
2 Ed's always buying presents for his friends. ____
3 Pablo hardly ever laughs. ____
4 Terri doesn't like meeting new people. ____
5 The children always remember to say "please" and "thank you." ____
6 George tells lies and tricks people. ____
7 Dad goes to the office on weekends! ____
8 My math teacher explains things carefully and never gets angry. ____

a serious
b hard-working
c shy
d dishonest
e polite
f mean
g patient
h generous

4 Complete the adjectives. The first letters are given.

1 My brother is a really im____________ person; he hates standing in line to pay.
2 Lola is so se____________that she only thinks about herself.
3 You can believe everything that Julia tells you; she's a very ho____________ person.
4 Ricardo never says hello to my parents when he comes to our house. They think he's r____________.
5 Marc is very so____________ ; he has lots of friends and often has parties at his house.
6 Hannah is so f____________ ; I never stop laughing when I'm with her.
7 Dan often helps me with jobs I need to do. He's very n__________.
8 Maria's so l____________ ; she stays in bed most of the day on the weekends!

PRONUNCIATION: Final *-s/-es* sound

5 1.1 Listen to the verb endings in these sentences. Check (✓) the correct column.

	/s/	/z/	/əz/
1 He wants to be a doctor.			
2 Silvia goes to college.			
3 Betty likes chocolate.			
4 Susie watches TV in the evenings.			
5 Paul changes clothes twice a day.			
6 Adam knows my brother.			
7 Lily thinks soccer is boring.			
8 Mr. Jones teaches us French.			

LISTENING: Listening for the main idea

1 1.2 Listen to Daniel and Laura's conversation. Are the sentences about Daniel true (T) or false (F)?

1 He wants to stop using his cell phone for a few weeks. ____
2 He wants to use his free time differently. ____
3 He wants to spend less time with other people. ____
4 He goes to the movies a lot. ____
5 He wants to go out more. ____
6 He doesn't want to spend any time in the kitchen. ____

2 1.2 Complete the sentences with the correct contractions. Then listen again and check.

1 So, Daniel, I hear you __________ going to use your phone this month.
2 At least, when __________ not at work.
3 I realized that I __________ actually do anything these days.
4 We never go out together these days. I mean, __________ crazy.
5 I __________ live my life like this!
6 I watch movies at home on my laptop instead. It __________ good.
7 Oh, and my __________ staying with me for a while.
8 __________ really good at baking.

3 Complete the sentences with the verbs in the box. There are two extra verbs.

stay collect play go on shop bake get go out spend get together with

1 He wants to __________ more time with his family.
2 She goes running three times a week to __________ in shape.
3 Do you often __________ your friends after work?
4 Some of the kids __________ chess at lunchtime.
5 In our free time we like to __________ cakes.
6 Do your parents __________ much exercise?
7 I don't __________ social media much.
8 They don't go to the shopping center. They prefer to __________ online.

GRAMMAR: Present continuous and simple present

1 Choose the correct options to complete the sentences.

1 Kathy can't go out today. ____ her essay.
a She's finishing b She finishes

2 This soup is very salty. ____ it.
a I'm not liking b I don't like

3 ____ a lot in your country?
a Is it snowing b Does it snow

4 ____ for exams right now.
a We're studying b We study

5 Is that Emir? ____ his brother.
a I'm knowing b I know

6 Sophia is busy. ____ dinner.
a She's cooking b She cooks

7 Luis works as a journalist. ____ articles about sports.
a He's writing b He writes

8 I can go with you. ____ anything right now.
a I'm not doing b I don't do

9 ____ his daughter to school every morning.
a Sam is taking b Sam takes

10 ____ to the gym with you very often?
a Is Raul going b Does Raul go

2 Complete the sentences with the simple present or present continuous form of the verbs in the box.

think not play walk do be work wear have

1 Mr. Silva ____________ past our house every morning.

2 Mom and Dad ____________ their lunch right now.

3 Laura ____________ in a café for three months this summer.

4 Luca ____________ soccer very often.

5 Olga and Sergei ____________ from Russia.

6 ____________ Helen usually ____________ her homework in the evenings?

7 Maria ____________ our new teacher is great.

8 Jorge ____________ a jacket today.

VOCABULARY: Useful verbs

3 Choose the correct verbs to complete the sentences.

1	I often ____ my keys. It's very annoying!	miss	lose
2	Pablo usually ____ our swimming races.	wins	earns
3	Susie ____ really happy, doesn't she?	looks like	looks
4	I'm cold! Let's ____ home.	go back	come back
5	Emma's ____ a blue coat today.	wearing	carrying
6	Can you ____ me to call Alan later?	remember	remind
7	I'm ____ for Francesca to arrive.	hoping	waiting
8	Are you ____ your vacation?	looking forward to	expecting
9	Emma often ____ me about her friends.	says	tells
10	I need to ____ some documents to Mr. Smith's office.	take	bring

4 Complete the conversation with verbs from exercise 3 in the correct tense.

Anna Are you going to Jorge and Sara's wedding? I'm really [1] ____________ it.
Laura Yes, I am! But I can only buy them a small present, because I'm not [2] ____________ very much money at the moment.
Anna Never mind! Do you have anything to wear to the wedding?
Laura No, but my sister [3] ____________ from her vacation tomorrow, and she has so many amazing dresses.
Anna I [4] ____________ she'll have something perfect!
Laura Yes, definitely. Every week she [5] ____________ home something new from the shopping center!
Anna By the way, do you [6] ____________ Carlos, Jorge's best friend?
Laura Yes, I do. He's the tall guy who [7] ____________ Zac Efron, isn't he? He's great—I really [8] ____________ he'll be at the wedding.
Anna Of course he will. Jorge [9] ____________ he's like a brother to him. He works in France in the winter, and Jorge really [10] ____________ him when he's gone.

PRONUNCIATION: *-ng* sound

5 1.3 Practice saying the sentences. Listen, check, and repeat.

1 I'm bringi**ng** Julio to the meeti**ng**.
2 He's studyi**ng** French in college.
3 She's carryi**ng** a you**ng** child.
4 Are they runni**ng** in the park?
5 They're singi**ng** my favorite so**ng**.
6 I'm taki**ng** a stro**ng** box for the heavy books.
7 She's weari**ng** a lo**ng** dress.

WRITING: Making notes

1 Read Cristina's blog about three important people in her life. Number the information for each person in the order it appears.

Bianca:
- **a** personality ____
- **b** relationship to Cristina ____
- **c** age ____

Clara Fuentes:
- **a** how she helped Cristina ____
- **b** her job ____
- **c** relationship to Cristina ____

Grandpa:
- **a** personality ____
- **b** relationship to Cristina's father ____
- **c** lifestyle ____

Lots of people say that their brothers and sisters are annoying, but I love being with my sister, Bianca. That's probably [1]__________ I don't live with her all the time! I'm away at college, but she's only six, [2]__________ our relationship is kind of different from most sisters. Bianca's really funny, and she makes me laugh a lot. When we go out, people sometimes think I'm her mom. I hope I have a daughter like her one day—but not yet!

The second person who is very important to me is my neighbor, Clara Fuentes. She has an unusual job for a woman [3]__________ she's an airline pilot. Clara told me once that women can do any job in the world! [4]__________ I'm studying engineering. There are only three women in my class, but I love it and I'm good at it.

Person number three is my grandpa, who is my dad's father. My dad has five brothers. [5]__________ our family is so big! Grandpa lives alone, but we all visit him, [6]__________ he's never lonely! He is interested in all of us, and always wants to know about our lives. He's very kind and generous and everyone loves him.

2 Complete 1–6 in the blog with *because*, *so*, or *That's why* and decide if each one is a reason or result.

3 Think of three important people in your life. Write notes about them.

	Person 1
name	
relationship to me	
his/her life: job, where they live, etc.	
his/her personality	
why he/she is important to me	

	Person 2
name	
relationship to me	
his/her life: job, where he/she lives, etc.	
his/her personality	
why he/she is important to me	

	Person 3
name	
relationship to me	
his/her life: job, where he/she lives, etc.	
his/her personality	
why he/she is important to me	

4 Write a blog about three important people in your life.

- Use some or all of your notes from exercise 3.
- Write as many ideas as you can about the main topics.
- Choose the best ideas and organize them into paragraphs.
- Include at least three sentences with *because*, *so*, or *That's why*.

HOME BLOG PODCASTS ABOUT CONTACT

Learning Curve

Tom and Sam talk about two friends, Paul and Adam.

LISTENING

1 1.4 Listen to the podcast. Check (✓) the things Paul talks about.

- **a** Adam's hobbies ____
- **b** how he met Adam ____
- **c** Adam's personality ____
- **d** what he has in common with Adam ____
- **e** Adam's children ____
- **f** where Paul lives ____

2 1.4 Listen again. Choose the correct options to complete the sentences.

1. Paul sees Adam
   - **a** most evenings.
   - **b** when they go running.
   - **c** at work.
2. Paul says that Adam
   - **a** enjoys going out.
   - **b** has a lot of friends.
   - **c** isn't very sociable.
3. Adam spends some of his free time
   - **a** playing games with his sons.
   - **b** playing sports with his sons.
   - **c** teaching his sons Spanish.
4. Paul and Adam
   - **a** always go to concerts with each other.
   - **b** belong to the same gym.
   - **c** like different types of music.
5. Paul says that Adam
   - **a** never talks about his friends.
   - **b** has the same job as Paul.
   - **c** helps Paul with his problems.
6. Adam
   - **a** is always very serious.
   - **b** makes Paul laugh.
   - **c** can sometimes be selfish.

READING

1 Read the blog about friendship. Check (✓) the correct sentence.

- **a** Teresa and Livia are about the same age. ____
- **b** Teresa and Livia have different jobs. ____
- **c** Teresa and Livia both have children. ____
- **d** Teresa isn't married. ____
- **e** Livia is Teresa's only friend. ____

2 Are the sentences true (T), false (F), or isn't there enough information to decide (N)?

1. According to the writer, nobody can be friends with someone who is 25 years older. ____
2. Teresa and Livia work in the same place. ____
3. They often spend time together. ____
4. Teresa thinks that Livia gets tired more often than Teresa. ____
5. Teresa has a lot of problems with her children. ____
6. Teresa discusses all her problems with her mother, too. ____
7. Teresa and Livia always like the same books. ____
8. Teresa learns more from Livia than Livia learns from Teresa. ____
9. Livia always likes the clothes that Teresa suggests for her. ____
10. Livia enjoys going out with Teresa. ____

HOME BLOG PODCASTS ABOUT CONTACT

Sam writes about friendship.

What're 25 years between friends?

What do you think of when you hear or use the phrase "best friend"? Probably two people of about the same age. When we think of relationships between older and younger people, we may have negative feelings about them. How often do we hear older people complaining that the young are lazy, selfish, and rude? Or young people saying that older people don't understand them? But does it have to be like that? Teresa Fuentes, 28, and Livia Robles, 53, say it doesn't!

Teresa

Livia and I work together in a large school. She works in the school office, and I'm a history teacher. We usually have lunch together, and sometimes we go out in the evenings, too. Livia may be 25 years older than me, but she's so much fun, and sometimes I think she has more energy than me! That's probably because I'm taking care of three small children, and her children are grown up.

I love having an older friend because Livia is always patient and she has a lot of life experience. She's interested in my life and gives me lots of good advice, especially about the kids. She's not afraid to be honest if she thinks I'm doing something wrong. I often talk to her about things I can't discuss with my mom because I don't want to worry her. But to me, Livia isn't like another mother—she's just Livia, my friend!

Livia

I think it's a really good thing to have friends of all ages. Talking to people with different lives and different experiences makes you think about things in a new way. Teresa and I often discuss the books we're reading, and it's interesting how different our opinions can be!

Teresa says she learns from me, but I learn a lot from her, too—about things like cooking and gardening. She and her husband grow all their own vegetables! She loves fashion too, and often suggests things for me that I wouldn't choose myself: This pink jacket I'm wearing now, for example.

And having a friend in her twenties means that I can go out and have fun. She even sometimes takes me to nightclubs! Being with Teresa and her friends reminds me of being young and, anyway, there's a lot more to life than housework and watching TV!

UNIT 2

Stories and pictures

2A LANGUAGE

GRAMMAR: Simple past and time expressions

1 Order the letters to make the simple past form of the verbs.

1 Anna usually rides her bike to work, but today she **kedlaw** ____________.
2 Daniel **okot** ____________ a bus to college yesterday.
3 Last night Marta **newt** ____________ to a concert.
4 Did you **grinb** ____________ any money with you?
5 We **ederbmerem** ____________ to send Tim a birthday card.
6 I **rited** ____________ to open the door, but it was locked.
7 Beatriz **retow** ____________ him a letter to explain the problem.
8 I **dretsta** ____________ my new job in January.
9 We **beldimc** ____________ to the top of the mountain.
10 Sara **tens** ____________ me an e-mail with the details.

2 Complete Rafael's postcard with the simple past of the verbs in parentheses.

Hi Mom and Dad!
We [1] ____________ *(get) here safely yesterday. The trip* [2] ____________ *(be) fine. Daniel's dad* [3] ____________ *(meet) us at the airport and* [4] ____________ *(drive) us to their house. In the evening we* [5] ____________ *(go) to the movies. On the way, we* [6] ____________ *(stop) at a café and* [7] ____________ *(have) some pizza. We* [8] ____________ *(get) home after midnight–I'm very tired today!*
Love from Rafael

VOCABULARY: *-ed/-ing* adjectives

3 Complete 1–6 with an adjective from each pair in the box.

amazed / amazing	annoyed / annoying	excited / exciting
confused / confusing	interested / interesting	tired / tiring

1 I'm ____________ by these instructions. They're not very clear.
2 My neighbors are ____________. They're so noisy.
3 Eric's brother is very ____________ in cars.
4 She's very ____________ about her vacation. She's really looking forward to it.
5 Ted felt ____________ after running ten kilometers.
6 We went to a fantastic restaurant last night. The food was ____________!

4 Complete the sentences with *-ed* or *-ing* adjectives.

1 I often fall asleep in my math classes. They're really b____________!
2 Betty was di____________ when she failed her driving test.
3 I'm su____________ to see Manuel. He doesn't usually come here.
4 Cristina's really te____________ of snakes, but her sister's not scared of them.
5 It's so em____________ when you can't remember someone's name!
6 We love spending the day at the beach. It's very re____________.

PRONUNCIATION: *-ed* endings

5 2.1 Listen and circle the sound that you hear at the end of the underlined verb. Listen, check, and repeat.

1 We climbed to the top of the mountain.	/t/	/əd/	/d/
2 I decided to go to Michael's house.	/t/	/əd/	/d/
3 Eduardo looked at the photograph.	/t/	/əd/	/d/
4 The cook experimented with new dishes.	/t/	/əd/	/d/
5 I traveled to Rome by train.	/t/	/əd/	/d/
6 In the evening, we watched TV.	/t/	/əd/	/d/
7 We opened our presents together.	/t/	/əd/	/d/
8 She worked all day yesterday.	/t/	/əd/	/d/

READING: Approaching a text

1 Read the title and the first three lines of the text. What do you think it is about?

- **a** A man who doesn't say much.
- **b** A man who isn't as quiet as people think.
- **c** A man who shouts a lot.

2 Look at the photograph. Who do you think the people are?

3 Match topics 1–4 with paragraph headings A–D.

1. A shy person doing something brave. ____
2. A couple getting married. ____
3. Something that is written down. ____
4. People wondering what someone will do. ____

The quiet man?

Robin Jones thought her grandfather was a quiet, shy man. Then she read her grandmother's diary and learned about the one time he wasn't ...

A All in black and white

Grandma's diary was about the year 1950. Every day she wrote about her life. Before June, it was mostly about her job at a jewelry store and the lives of the other young women who worked there. But after June, she started to mention a regular customer—a nice young man who came in to buy a necklace for his mother. Then he came back the next day, and the next, and the next ...

B Will he, won't he?

Each time, he asked Grandma to help him, but he never bought anything else. Eventually, one of the other salespeople said to Grandma, "I know why he comes. It's to see you!" They all expected Grandpa to ask her out, but he never did.

C The mouse becomes a lion

Then one day everything changed. Grandpa was in the store when a man ran in with a gun. He pointed it at Grandma and told her to give him a diamond ring. In an instant, that shy young man changed. "Drop the gun!" he shouted, and pushed the man to the floor. "Don't you dare frighten that young woman! She's going to be my wife one day!"

D Wedding bells

After that, the police came and arrested the robber, and everyone said that Grandpa was a hero. But there was something Grandma still wasn't sure about. "Did you just ask me to marry you?" she asked Grandpa. Grandpa just smiled, but two months later they got married!

4 Are the sentences true (T) or false (F)?

1. Grandma wrote about Grandpa before June. ____
2. Grandpa bought lots of jewelry from the store. ____
3. The other salespeople thought Grandpa liked Grandma. ____
4. The robber tried to steal a necklace from the store. ____
5. Grandpa was very angry with the robber. ____
6. The police took the robber away. ____
7. The people in the store thought Grandpa was brave. ____
8. Grandma always knew that Grandpa wanted to marry her. ____

5 Complete the sentences about the text with *then*, *after*, or *later*.

1. ____________ Robin Jones read her grandmother's diary, she had a different idea about her grandfather.
2. One day, Grandpa came to the store to buy a necklace. A day ____________, he came into the store again.
3. ____________ that, Grandma started to write about him in her diary.
4. ____________ a while, the other salespeople realized that Grandpa was coming to see Grandma.
5. A man pointed a gun at Grandma. ____________ he tried to steal a ring.
6. A few minutes ____________, the police arrived.

GRAMMAR: Question forms

1 Order the words to make questions.

1 did / do / what / on vacation / they
______________________________?
2 need / we / to buy / do / a ticket
______________________________?
3 did / the movies / who / with / go to / Bruno
______________________________?
4 is / apartment / where / new / Sally's
______________________________?
5 do / how / to / the station / get / you
______________________________?
6 do / dinner / you / want / what / for
______________________________?
7 the milk / in / is / the refrigerator
______________________________?
8 play / does / sister / the violin / your
______________________________?

2 Complete the questions to match the answers. Write one or two words in each space.

1 __________ are you __________?
I'm from Peru.
2 __________ is your English teacher?
Mrs. Smith is my English teacher.
3 __________ you __________ Max today?
No, I didn't see Max today.
4 __________ you move to New York?
I moved to New York in 2015.
5 __________ his name?
His name is Louis.
6 __________ Maria a teacher?
Yes, she is.
7 __________ Larry very angry?
No, Larry wasn't very angry.
8 __________ you travel to Lima?
We traveled to Lima by plane.

VOCABULARY: Life stages

3 Read about Kazuo's life. Order the phrases. Write 1–6.

a engaged to Eriko ____
b children (two boys) ____
c retired 1990 ____
d born Kyoto, 1930 ____
e married Eriko ____
f elementary and middle school, Tokyo ____

4 Complete the text about Kazuo's life. Write one word in each space.

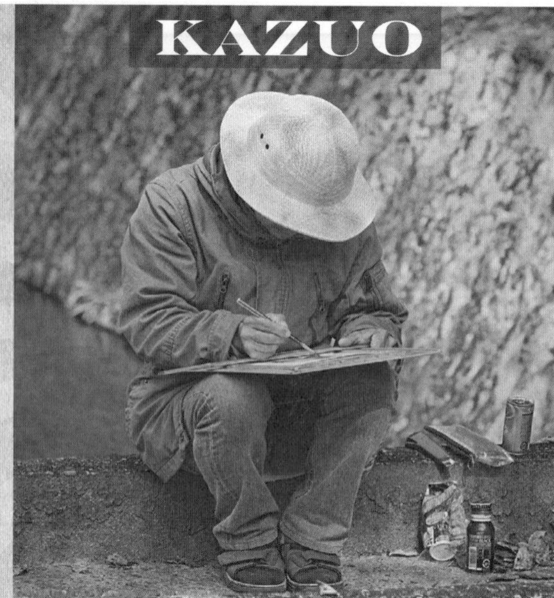

Kazuo [1]__________ born in Kyoto, in Japan, in 1930. His family moved when he was still a baby and he grew [2]__________ in Tokyo, where he [3]__________ to elementary and middle school. After Kazuo [4]__________ high school, he [5]__________ to college to study medicine. At the university, he met a girl named Eriko. They [6]__________ engaged, but they waited until graduating from college before they [7]__________ married. They [8]__________ two children. Kazuo worked as a doctor for 30 years. In 1990, after a successful career, he [9]__________ and spent the next twenty years doing what he loved: painting. Sadly, Kazuo [10]__________ in 2015, at the age of 85.

PRONUNCIATION: Question intonation

5 2.2 Listen to the questions. Does the intonation go up (U) or down (D) at the end?

1 How do you spell your name? ____
2 Do you like cheese? ____
3 Is their house very big? ____
4 When is her birthday? ____
5 Where do you live? ____
6 Did you see Peter? ____
7 Was Anna very angry? ____
8 Who did you go on vacation with? ____

SPEAKING: Telling a personal story

1 2.3 Listen to Emma tell Dominic a personal story. Check (✓) the phrases you hear.

- **a** What happened? ____
- **b** Did I ever tell you about the time …? ____
- **c** That's amazing! ____
- **d** Really? ____
- **e** What did you do then? ____
- **f** Oh no! ____
- **g** You're joking! ____
- **h** That's awful! ____
- **i** That reminds me of … ____
- **j** Lucky you! ____
- **k** You poor thing! ____
- **l** You'll never guess … ____
- **m** I felt really … ____

2 2.3 Listen again. Which of the phrases in exercise 1 do Emma and Dominic use to do these things?

1. Emma tells Dominic something surprising. ____
2. Dominic shows sympathy. ____ ____ ____
3. Emma describes her emotions after the accident happened. ____
4. Dominic shows that he is interested. ____
5. Dominic says that something similar happened to him. ____

3 2.4 Listen to six people talking. Choose the best way of showing interest and say it aloud.

1. *You poor thing! / What did he do then? / That's amazing!*
2. *What happened? / Oh no! / Lucky you!*
3. *Great! / That's awful! / You're joking!*
4. *What did he do then? / You poor thing! / Great!*
5. *What happened? / Lucky you! / Oh no!*
6. *That's amazing! / That's awful! / What happened?*

4 2.5 Listen and check your answers to exercise 3.

5 2.6 Match the sentence parts. Say them aloud. Then listen and check.

1. Something similar ____
2. That reminds ____
3. You'll never guess ____
4. Let me ____
5. Can you ____
6. I felt ____
7. Did I ever tell ____
8. It was ____

- **a** nervous about meeting her.
- **b** tell you about my flight to Tokyo.
- **c** you about the time I met Zac Efron?
- **d** so amazing to discover we have the same name!
- **e** imagine how scared I was?
- **f** happened to me when I was a student.
- **g** what happened to Regina yesterday.
- **h** me of the time I lost my passport.

Learning Curve

HOME BLOG PODCASTS ABOUT CONTACT

Tom and Sam talk about an embarrassing moment.

LISTENING

1 2.7 Listen to the podcast. Choose the best summary.

- **a** Maria made friends with an old lady.
- **b** Maria dropped someone's bag on the train.
- **c** Maria upset a complete stranger.

2 2.7 Listen again. Choose the correct options to complete the sentences.

1 Maria was surprised by
- **a** how old the lady was.
- **b** how nice the lady looked.
- **c** how interesting the lady was.

2 Maria and the lady had
- **a** nothing to talk about.
- **b** little to talk about.
- **c** a lot to talk about.

3 When she stood up, the lady appeared
- **a** shorter.
- **b** younger.
- **c** older.

4 Maria tried to help the lady by
- **a** supporting her with her arm.
- **b** supporting her with her arm and holding her bag.
- **c** holding her bag.

5 Maria dropped the lady's
- **a** candy.
- **b** bag.
- **c** stick.

6 The bag fell on
- **a** the track.
- **b** the platform.
- **c** a man.

7 The old lady was
- **a** very angry.
- **b** pretty calm.
- **c** too upset to talk.

8 The man helped them by
- **a** mending the bag.
- **b** picking up the medicine bottle.
- **c** getting the bag back.

READING

1 Read the blog about games that use pictures. Complete 1–6 with the adjectives in the box.

annoyed	disappointing	confusing
surprised	interesting	boring

2 Are the sentences true (T), false (F), or isn't there enough information to decide (N)?

1 The writer's family plays games together every Christmas. ____

2 The writer's sister got more correct answers than their father. ____

3 The writer's mother couldn't name any of the famous people. ____

4 The Spot the Ball competition started in the 1970s. ____

5 The writer's mother played Spot the Ball more than once. ____

6 The writer's father was angry when his wife won a prize. ____

7 The writer's parents didn't earn much money. ____

8 Spot the Ball is less popular today than in the past. ____

9 Spot the Ball is a more difficult competition today than in the 1970s. ____

10 The writer prefers games that use pictures of animals. ____

HOME BLOG PODCASTS ABOUT CONTACT

Tom writes about his favorite games.

Games that use pictures

I'm an amateur photographer, so it's probably not surprising that I love games that are based on images. Last Christmas I organized a quiz for my family. I selected images of different people in the news that year and everyone earned a point for each person they could name correctly. My sister thought it was [1]___________, so she didn't really try. I was really [2]___________ when my dad won. He even managed to recognize Taylor Swift!

Then my parents told me about a game named "Spot the Ball" that was very popular in the 1970s. It was a simple game found in lots of newspapers. You looked at an action shot of a soccer game, but the ball was removed from the photo, and you had to say where you thought it should be. Apparently, my dad found it really [3]___________ and played it every week. But Mom got very [4]___________ with him because he wanted to discuss exactly where all the players were looking. Mom used to guess, and one week she won! She only won $100, but that was a lot of money in those days.

Later, I read an article about the game, and I was amazed that the last time anyone won the jackpot prize, was in 2004! About three million people used to play it every week in the 1970s, but now there are only about 14,000 players. I think that's a little [5]___________ because it's a lot of fun.

There's another game that I really enjoy that uses images. You see a very small part of something in detail. and you have to figure out what it is. There are entire blogs with these kinds of pictures; one of my favorites is *http://floorsix.blogspot.co.uk/* . Some of the images are really [6]___________, but to me, that's what makes them even more interesting. I love asking myself questions about them: What does it look like? Is it an animal? Is that part of a machine? How big is it really? Do you want to take a guess? Look at these three images and try to figure out what they are.

UNIT 3

Keep on traveling.

3A LANGUAGE

GRAMMAR: Comparatives, superlatives, *(not) as ... as*

1 Choose the correct options to complete the sentences.

1 The weather here is hotter _____ it is in Germany.
a most b than c as

2 My sister isn't _____ tall as me.
a as b than c more

3 This sofa is _____ comfortable than the other one.
a most b as c more

4 Matias is the _____ boy in our class!
a funniest b more funny c funnier

5 For me, science is _____ class of all!
a the most bad b worst c the worst

6 Is your house _____ Rafael's?
a as big than b as big as
c more big than

7 Stella makes _____ best cakes in the world!
a most b the c as

8 This is the _____ expensive restaurant in the city.
a most b as c more

2 Complete the conversation with comparative and superlative forms of the adjectives in the box.

far cheap early important lazy
close crowded interesting

A Hi, Daniel. I heard you moved to a new apartment.

B Yes, I moved downtown because I wanted to be [1]_____________ to work. Taking public transportation was so expensive. I can walk everywhere now, which is a lot [2]_____________.

A I know! I live even [3]_____________ away than you did. It costs so much, and I think it's the [4]_____________ train in the country; it's always completely full in the mornings.

B Maybe you should move, as well! I find living downtown a lot [5]_____________ than living in the suburbs. There's so much to do here.

A I could never live downtown. My pets are the [6]_____________ things in my life. I couldn't live without them!

B Maybe you should try taking an [7]_____________ train?

A Probably, but I hate getting up in the morning. I'm the [8]_____________ member of my family!

VOCABULARY: Useful adjectives

3 Order the letters to make adjectives.

1 I didn't sleep well because the hotel bed was so FRONTBAUMCELO. _____________

2 I need to pack my suitcase again because it's too SYSEM. _____________

3 I didn't think the beach would be so TIQUE on the weekend. _____________

4 Athens is NICETAN. People have lived there for over 7,000 years. _____________

5 The Eiffel Tower is the most SOMAFU building in Paris. _____________

6 His store sells LUNUSUA souvenirs that you won't find anywhere else. _____________

4 Complete the text about Tokyo. The first letters are given.

With nearly 40 million people living there, Tokyo is one of the most [1] c __ __ __ __ __ __ cities in the world. And it has more cars than anywhere else in Japan, almost 70 million of them, so it's extremely [2] p __ __ __ __ __ __ __, as well. But Tokyo is also one of the most popular places for foreign tourists to visit. It's very safe and, although it's extremely [3] b __ __ __, many people love the fact that it's really [4] l __ __ __ __ __ and that there's plenty to see and do. Some visitors may think that [5] m __ __ __ __ __ __ buildings like the Sugamo-Shinkin bank, built in 2011, are [6] u __ __ __, but others think they are beautiful and love the fact that they use some of the best 21st century technology.

PRONUNCIATION: Sentence stress

5 3.1 Circle the underlined word that is most stressed. Listen, check, and repeat.

1 Albert is the <u>best</u> student in <u>his</u> class.
2 My <u>soup</u> doesn't taste as <u>good</u> as Jasmine's.
3 Tokyo is <u>closer</u> to Mumbai <u>than</u> to São Paulo.
4 Is <u>Lady</u> Gaga more <u>famous</u> than Taylor Swift?
5 <u>My</u> car is the most <u>expensive</u> thing I own.
6 Sophia's essay <u>was</u> a lot <u>better</u> than Helena's.
7 It's <u>quieter</u> in the country than <u>in</u> the city.
8 I'm feeling <u>a</u> little <u>happier</u> than I was before.

LISTENING: Identifying key points

1 3.2 Listen to Joe and Sara talking about vacations. Are the sentences true (T) or false (F)?

1. Sara visits a lot of cities. _____
2. Joe and Sara don't enjoy the same types of vacations. _____
3. Sara doesn't like traveling alone. _____

2 3.2 Listen again and choose the correct words to complete the sentences.

1. Sara really likes *cities* / *beaches* / *hotels*.
2. Joe doesn't enjoy *going to the beach* / *going hiking* / *going abroad*.
3. Sara doesn't like *museums* / *sunbathing* / *churches*.
4. A week before Sara leaves, she *makes hotel reservations* / *packs her suitcase* / *books a flight*.
5. The night before Sara leaves, she *plans her sightseeing* / *eats out* / *packs a suitcase*.
6. Sara spends most of her vacation *by herself* / *with other people* / *on guided tours*.
7. Sara likes traveling alone because she can *choose what to do* / *read more* / *go sightseeing*.
8. Sara takes a book when she *goes sightseeing* / *eats out by herself* / *goes on guided tours*.

3 3.3 Underline the key words that are most likely to be stressed by the speaker in these sentences. Listen and check.

1. The museums are crowded in the summer.
2. Did you book a flight?
3. We could rent a car at the airport.
4. I'd love to travel abroad.
5. The barbecue at the hotel was fantastic.
6. They stay in a beautiful house by the ocean.

4 Complete the sentences with the correct form of the verbs in the box.

reserve	buy	eat out	go
have	rent	visit	stay

1. We both love to _____________ at the local restaurants.
2. Could you _____________ a double room for my parents, please?
3. Let's _____________ a car to drive around the island.
4. My little sister likes to _____________ a few souvenirs to take home.
5. My aunt and uncle usually _____________ camping in the summer.
6. Lucy and James are _____________ at a beach resort.
7. Today we _____________ the local attractions.
8. Peter always _____________ a great time when he's on vacation.

GRAMMAR: Past continuous and simple past

1 Order the words to make sentences. Add commas where necessary.

1 Alba was / café when / waiting / I arrived / in the

______________________________.

2 working when / Nancy / was / I / her / left

______________________________.

3 taking / called / Sara / When Lara / a shower / was

______________________________.

4 he was / Ed lived / at home while / studying / law

______________________________.

5 I looked / was smiling / that he / at Dad / and saw

______________________________.

6 still waiting / were / to get in / When the show / started / we

______________________________.

7 her homework / book while / Marian was / I read a / finishing

______________________________.

8 into the / we were / house while / The thieves / got / sleeping

______________________________.

9 watching TV / cooking while / were / Mom was / the kids

______________________________.

10 shopping her friend / While Paola was / went to / the museum

______________________________.

2 Complete each sentence with the verbs in parentheses. Write one past continuous and one simple past form.

1 When we __________ Carlos, he __________ his car. (see, clean)

2 Marta __________ for the bus when she __________. (run, fall)

3 Anna __________ Julia while she __________ to class. (meet, walk)

4 Hugo __________ his leg when he __________ tennis. (hurt, play)

5 My phone __________ while I __________. (ring, drive)

6 When Rick __________ his hair, he __________ shampoo in his eyes. (wash, get)

7 Emma __________ late for class because she __________ to Luisa. (be, talk)

8 The plane __________ above the ocean when the storm __________. (fly, start)

9 My sister __________ my phone when I __________. (take, not look)

10 When Jackie __________ her shopping, someone __________ her bag. (do, steal)

PRONUNCIATION: *was/were*

3 3.4 Practice saying the sentences. Pay attention to the pronunciation of *was* /wəz/ and *were* /wər/. Listen, check, and repeat.

1 What were you doing at five o'clock yesterday?

2 I was expecting Monica to call.

3 Rafael was talking to his friend.

4 We were playing outside, but it started to rain.

5 Adam was watching TV while I worked.

6 While you were sleeping, I baked a cake.

7 I was doing my homework all morning.

8 Clara was running when the accident happened.

WRITING: Writing a narrative

1 Read two paragraphs from different parts of a story about a vacation incident. Choose the correct verbs.

A They went up to the check—in desk, where a woman [1]*checked / was checking* everyone's tickets and passports. Simon [2]*gave / was giving* her their passports. The woman took them, then looked at Simon strangely. "Why did you give me this?" she asked. Then Simon and Gabrielle [3]*got / were getting* a terrible shock. They didn't have Gabrielle's passport. They had Simon's passport and Simon's old passport!

B Simon and Gabrielle sat in the car. They felt happy and were talking to Simon's brother, Toby, who [4]*drove / was driving* them to the airport for their skiing trip. They had to be there by 5:30 a.m., and there weren't any buses that early. They were tired, but excited. They had a good trip and Toby [5]*left / was leaving* them outside the airport. They thanked him and [6]*went / were going* to get their flight.

2 Read two more paragraphs from different parts of the story. Choose the correct adjectives or adverbs.

C However, when she got back, the airline staff was very [1]*helpful / helpfully*. They [2]*kind / kindly* found her a seat on a later flight and she didn't have to pay extra. When she arrived in Denver, the shuttle to the ski resort had already left, but it was easy to get a bus there. She arrived in time for a [3]*delicious / deliciously* dinner, and she quickly forgave Simon. After all, anyone can make a mistake and everything worked out in the end!

D The woman told them rather [4]*rude / rudely* that Gabrielle couldn't travel. She said that Simon should get on the plane. "But he's the one who made the mistake!" said Gabrielle. She was really angry. However, there was nothing they could do. Gabrielle had to rent a car and drive back home for her passport. It was a fast trip, but she still missed the flight. She felt very worried and [5]*miserable / miserably*.

3 Look at these sentences from the text. Rewrite them using adverbs instead of adjectives.

1. They felt happy and were talking.
   They talked ____________.
2. They had a good trip.
   The trip went ____________.
3. "But he's the one who made the mistake!" said Gabrielle. She was really angry.
   "But he's the one who made the mistake!" said Gabrielle ____________.
4. It was a fast trip, but she still missed the flight.
   She drove ____________, but she still missed the flight.

4 Match 1–4 with paragraphs A–D.

1. The background (who, when, where) ____
2. A problem (what happened) ____
3. A resolution (how she solved the problem) ____
4. The ending (what happened in the end, how she felt) ____

5 Write a different last paragraph for the story.

- Use the ideas below or your own ideas.
- Write at least five sentences.
- Use the past continuous and the simple past correctly.
- Use adjectives and adverbs to make your paragraph more interesting.

no plane until next day

went to wrong ski resort

Simon was waiting for her at the airport in Denver

decided to stay home and not go skiing

had a big argument with Simon

had to pay for a new ticket

HOME BLOG PODCASTS ABOUT CONTACT

Tom and Sam talk about working abroad.

LISTENING

1 3.5 Listen to the podcast. Circle True or False.

1	Mara worked with elephants in Thailand.	True	False
2	She found the work fairly easy.	True	False
3	The local people weren't very friendly.	True	False
4	Mara went to Thailand by herself.	True	False
5	One of the animals got sick.	True	False

2 3.5 Listen again. Complete the sentences with a maximum of three words.

1. Mara says it was ____________ to be so close to the animals.
2. Mara enjoyed being part of a ____________.
3. The ____________ made the work difficult for Mara.
4. Mara really enjoyed eating the ____________.
5. Some of the people Mara worked with went to Thailand in ____________.
6. Mara made ____________ with people from around the world.
7. Mara says it's important to ____________ a lot there because of the heat.
8. Mara felt better after someone gave her a large ____________.

READING

1 Read the blog about four hotels. What do you think the word "quirkiest" in the heading means?

a most expensive
b most comfortable
c most unusual
d most famous

2 Match the descriptions to hotels A–D.

1. It is a very unusual shape. ____
2. It is difficult to get into. ____
3. It has no walls or roof. ____
4. It is made of a substance not normally used for buildings. ____

3 Choose the correct options to complete the sentences.

1. The Palacio de Sal is in an area
   a where salt is produced.
   b where many tourists want to go.
   c without normal building materials.
2. According to the blog, the restaurant at the Palacio de Sal
   a makes the best food in Bolivia.
   b makes food that is too salty.
   c makes a popular dish with salt.
3. Jules' Undersea Lodge is
   a in deep water.
   b only reached by taxi.
   c in shallow water.
4. People with heart problems can't stay at Jules' Undersea Lodge because
   a doctors can't reach the hotel.
   b it's not comfortable enough.
   c it is not safe for them.
5. In Dog Bark Park Inn, the beds are
   a in rooms in the dog.
   b shaped like dogs.
   c all in one big room.
6. At Dog Bark Park Inn, real dogs
   a have to be kept inside always.
   b are allowed to stay.
   c are not welcome.
7. According to the blog, it is good to stay in a treehouse because
   a you can stay outside all night.
   b you can see unusual animals.
   c it is cheaper than a hotel.
8. According to the blog, sleeping outside means you can experience
   a being with other people.
   b other aspects of nature.
   c waking up very early.

HOME BLOG PODCASTS ABOUT CONTACT

Guest blogger Simon writes about hotels.

The world's best places to stay

Four of the world's quirkiest hotels

What do you want from a hotel? Something clean and comfortable for sure, but do you sometimes find your hotel room a little boring? Do you want your nights to be as much a part of your vacation adventure as your days? Here are four recommendations for a stay you'll never forget!

A Palacio de Sal

Most of us know about the ice hotels in countries like Sweden, where everything, even your bed, is made out of ice. But this hotel in Bolivia is even more unusual; it is made out of salt! About 350 km. south of the city of La Paz, this hotel is on the edge of the Salar de Uyuni, the world's largest salt plain. It was built using around a million blocks of salt. Visitors report that the food in the restaurant is excellent, especially their famous "salt chicken." There's even a swimming pool, filled with salt water, of course!

B Jules' Undersea Lodge

Usually you can get a taxi to your hotel, but not here! To stay in this hotel in Key Largo, you need to scuba dive to reach the entrance. Once you're there, you can watch fish through the windows of your room. Amazingly, there are hot showers, and you can even get pizza delivered! Because you have to dive to get to the lodge, you need to be in good shape. If you have heart problems, or are pregnant, this isn't the place for you!

C Dog Bark Park Inn

This has to be one of the strangest-looking hotels in the world. Owned by a husband and wife team in Idaho, U.S. the entire hotel looks like a large wooden dog! Four people can sleep inside the dog. There's even a room in its head. Rooms are filled with doggy decorations, and pets are, of course, welcome to stay with you!

D Chalkley's Treehouse

A safari is all about being outdoors, isn't it? It's all about the animals and the wide open spaces. So why go into a building or a tent at night when you could stay under the stars in this treehouse on the Lion Sands Game Reserve in South Africa? You can lie in bed and look up at the stars, watch the sun come up in the morning, and listen to the sound of animals and birds all around you. What could be more romantic?

UNIT 4

The working world

4A LANGUAGE

GRAMMAR: *will*, *may*, and *might* for predictions

1 Read the statements. How likely is it that these things will happen? Write 1–8 in the correct columns.

1 Phelps will win the swimming competition.
2 She might lose the tennis match.
3 I don't think I will ever travel into space.
4 We might not finish the project on time.
5 They won't finish the work by Friday.
6 We may be able to go camping.
7 Of course, I may not get the job.
8 He'll get there before lunchtime.

Probably (More than 75%)	Possibly (50–75%)	Possibly not (25–50%)	Probably not (Less than 25%)
____	____	____	____
____	____	____	____

2 Complete the sentences with *will, won't, might, think,* or *don't think*.

1 I know for sure that Fatima ____________ come to the party; she promised she would.
2 Gabriel ____________ be home by six o'clock. It depends how much work he has to do.
3 I ____________ Bernie will come to the movies. He's too busy.
4 He definitely ____________ come with us on Tuesday. He only goes out on the weekends.
5 I ____________ Victor will pass his exam. He's so smart and he's been studying hard.
6 We ____________ go to the park for a picnic, although it depends on the weather.
7 I may visit Fernanda this evening, so I probably ____________ go to the concert after all.
8 Don't worry, we ____________ definitely get to the restaurant on time!
9 The sky looks fairly blue. I ____________ that it'll rain today.
10 Our project is going very well, so we ____________ it'll be a success.

VOCABULARY: Jobs

3 Order the letters to complete the names of the jobs.

1 salesSNREPO ____________
2 soccer OCCAH ____________
3 fashion SEDGINRE ____________
4 movie RIDECROT ____________
5 police FOFCIER ____________
6 tour UGIED ____________
7 security UDARG ____________
8 travel TEGAN ____________

4 Complete the jobs. Some of the letters are given.

1 I asked an ac____________ for some advice about my money.
2 Luckily, the f____________s put out the fire very quickly.
3 We needed a l____________ to help us understand the contract.
4 Are all the fruit and vegetables at the market grown by local f____________?
5 She got her h____________ to cut her hair a lot shorter.
6 He's a well-known j____________ and writes for the national newspapers.
7 My cousin's a fashion m____________; she works for all the big designers.
8 We were given our room keys by the r____________ at the hotel.
9 Tomorrow I'll meet the s____________ who's going to operate on my knee.
10 Could you ask the w____________r to bring us some water with our meal?

PRONUNCIATION: *want/won't*

5 ▶ 4.1 Look at the underlined letters and listen to the sentences. Write 1 if the sound is /o/ and 2 if the sound is /a/. Listen, check, and repeat.

1 They use r<u>o</u>bots in the factory. ____
2 I really w<u>a</u>nt to see that movie. ____
3 I d<u>o</u>n't like cheese at all. ____
4 Do you kn<u>o</u>w where he lives? ____
5 My b<u>o</u>ss will be at the party tonight. ____
6 Isaac is looking for a j<u>o</u>b. ____
7 Manuel's mother used to be a m<u>o</u>del. ____
8 How <u>o</u>ld is your sister? ____

READING: Skimming a text

1 Read topic sentences A–E in the article. Match each one with the most likely summary 1–5.

1 Evidence from a piece of research. ____
2 The value of time away from work. ____
3 How to reduce our use of handheld devices. ____
4 How technology affects our behavior. ____
5 Tips to help you concentrate. ____

A We're all multitaskers now, performing two or more tasks at the same time. Whether it's e-mailing a colleague while checking our smartphone, or writing an essay while catching up on the latest online celebrity gossip, we're all doing it. But should we? Well, recent research suggests it's time to stop demanding so much of our brain and go back to focusing on one thing at a time.

B Consider the results of a study of workers at a software company. When they stopped working on a major task to answer an e-mail or message, it took ten minutes to be able to fully concentrate again on the original task. Clearly this is not an efficient way of working. Training ourselves to concentrate isn't easy, but psychologist Maria Sylva has some tips:

C Let your mind focus on one thing at a time. Whatever task you're doing, make sure you give it your full attention. Giving 100% to the task in hand will help you work more quickly and more accurately. At the beginning, this might be tough, so start with short periods, say ten minutes, and gradually increase the amount of time.

D If your smartphone is the main source of distraction, leave it at home. If you really believe the next message you receive will be more interesting or important than your current activity, ask yourself why you are doing that activity.

E Give your brain a rest. You'll achieve more if, several times a day, you walk away from tasks that require concentration. And I mean "walk away." Don't just look away from your screen or stare out of the window. Get up and leave your desk. If possible, get some fresh air. Taking a complete break will help your brain to come up with new ideas.

2 Read the whole article, then choose the best ending for each sentence.

1 Maria Sylva wants us to consider whether
  a technology is a good thing in our lives.
  b we should be doing so many things at once.
  c we should use smartphones.
2 The study that she refers to shows that we lose time when we
  a change the task we are working on.
  b only use e-mail to communicate at work.
  c don't concentrate hard enough at work.
3 She claims we make fewer mistakes when we
  a work quickly.
  b work for ten minutes at a time.
  c concentrate fully on a task.
4 She tells us not to take a smartphone with us if
  a the messages we get on it are not interesting.
  b it prevents us from giving attention to what we are doing.
  c we leave the house.
5 She recommends
  a putting off tasks that need us to concentrate.
  b taking regular short breaks from work.
  c looking away from our screens occasionally.

3 Complete the text with the correct pronouns and possessive adjectives.

Maria Sylva is a life coach. 1 ____________ advises people on how to manage 2 ____________ time. Most of 3 ____________ work is done inside companies where she coaches people at all levels, helping 4 ____________ perform to the best of their ability while 5 ____________ are working. Maria thoroughly enjoys her job and finds 6 ____________ very satisfying. Her aim is to help 7 ____________ accomplish the most that we possibly can during 8 ____________ working day.

GRAMMAR: *be going to* and present continuous

1 Choose the correct options to complete the sentences.

1 Pablo *going to study / is going to study / studying* medicine next year.
2 What *do you do / you doing / are you doing* this weekend?
3 I *going to / 'm going to / go to* finish my book tonight.
4 We're *visiting / visit / to visit* my parents next weekend.
5 I'm *meeting / meet / to meet* Daniel and Julia this evening if you'd like to join us.
6 We *going to / 're going to / 're going* buy our tickets tomorrow.
7 I *go to / 'm going to / going to* go running in half an hour.
8 My brother *is going to / is going to be / is being* at the festival.
9 Where *do you stay / are you staying / you stay* in Italy this summer?
10 I *go to / 'm going to / going to* ask Nancy if she wants to come to the theater.

2 Complete the sentences with the verbs in the box. Use the form in parentheses.

paint bake speak start see rent

1 I can give Mary that book for you. I ____________ her next week. (present continuous)
2 I think I ____________ to Lily about the problem. (*be going to*)
3 I've decided I ____________ a picture of my grandma's garden for her birthday. (*be going to*)
4 I'll be in Portugal for six months. I ____________ an apartment in Lisbon. (present continuous)
5 I ____________ a cake for Maria's birthday. (*be going to*)
6 Ismael ____________ a new job in July. (present continuous)

VOCABULARY: Phrases about work

3 Match the two parts of the sentences.

1 I want to accept the job, but first we have to agree on ____
2 She's so unhappy at work. I think she's going to quit ____
3 The interview went well, so I really hope I get ____
4 Think about the questions they might ask before you go on ____
5 The first step in applying for a job is to send in the application ____
6 Henry is hoping that he's going to get a pay ____
7 Larry is going to show me how to write ____
8 You must be looking forward to starting ____

a her job.
b an interview.
c form.
d a salary.
e a résumé.
f a job offer.
g work.
h raise.

4 Complete the text about Lucas's job. The first letters are given.

Lucas started a [1] c____________ in nursing five years ago. In January, he saw an [2] a____________ for a job at the local hospital and decided to [3] a____________ for it. They invited him to an [4] i____________ which went very well. Two weeks later, they made him a job [5] o____________. Before he started work, he had to [6] t____________ a training course to improve his skills. Lucas is obviously great at his job. He has already received a [7] p____________, and he now has more responsibility and earns a big [8] s____________. In fact, he earns much more than I do!

PRONUNCIATION: *going to* and *want to*

5 4.2 Listen to the sentences. Pay attention to the pronunciation of *going to* and *want to*. Listen again and repeat.

1 I'm going to apply for that position.
2 I want to quit this job.
3 I don't want to work in an office.
4 She's going to ask for a pay raise.
5 They're going to offer it to her.
6 He's going to write a résumé.

SPEAKING: Telephone language

1 4.3 Listen to a telephone conversation between Anne, who runs a company that offers disco lights and music for parties, and Ryan, a hotel receptionist. Number the phrases in the order you hear them.

- **a** Could you ask him to call me back, please? ____
- **b** Hello, … ____
- **c** I'm afraid he's not available right now. ____
- **d** How can I help you? ____
- **e** Thanks for calling. ____
- **f** Could I speak to …? ____
- **g** Can I take a message? ____
- **h** Can you tell him that …? ____

2 Complete the chart with options a–h from exercise 1.

Caller	Person being called
____	____
____	____
____	____
	____
	____

3 4.4 Complete the conversation with phrases for dealing with difficulties. Then listen and check.

A Good morning, Hobson's department store. This is Helen. How can I help you?

B Hello, could I speak to someone in the electrical department, please?

A Sorry, could you [1] ____________ a little louder? This line's really bad. And [2] ____________ speak more slowly, please?

B Yes, I'd like to speak to someone in the electrical department, please.

A Of course. I'll put you through to Simon Jones. He's in charge of electrical goods.

… Oh, I'm sorry. I'm afraid he's not available right now. He'll be back at eleven o'clock.

B Sorry, did [3] ____________ eleven?

A That's right. Should I ask him to call you?

B Yes, please. My number is 0755 511817.

A Could you [4] ____________, please?

B Yes, it's 0755 511817. Oh, and could you tell him that it needs to be as small as possible because I don't have much shelf space in my bedroom?

A I'm afraid I [5] ____________ that.

B Don't worry, I'll tell him when he calls.

A OK. And can I take your name, please?

B Robert Faux.

A Can [6] ____________ that, please?

B F-A-U-X.

A [7] ____________ A-U or E-U?

B A-U.

A Great, thank you. Simon will call you later. Goodbye.

Learning Curve

HOME BLOG PODCASTS ABOUT CONTACT

Tom and Sam talk about career changes.

LISTENING

1 4.5 Listen to the podcast. Choose the correct statement.

- **a** Larissa had problems at work and was extremely unhappy.
- **b** Larissa didn't want to do the same thing forever.
- **c** Larissa hated being an accountant and prefers being a teacher.

2 4.5 Listen again. Are the sentences true (T) or false (F)?

1. Larissa earned a lot of money as an accountant. ____
2. The people she worked with were much younger than her. ____
3. She found an interesting job advertisement in a newspaper. ____
4. She was very surprised when she got the job. ____
5. She loved her time on the island. ____
6. She does not have definite plans for the future. ____
7. She might work as an accountant again. ____
8. She's definitely going to use her teaching skills in her next job. ____

READING

1 Read the blog about seven different careers. Match descriptions A–G with these jobs.

1. accountant ____
2. fashion designer ____
3. hairdresser ____
4. journalist ____
5. lawyer ____
6. receptionist ____
7. salesperson ____

2 Match each person with the job (A–G) that would be most suitable.

1. Evie is a patient and hardworking person. She enjoys talking to people and she always dresses well; her appearance is really important to her! ____
2. Jamie has a great imagination. He has always been good at art and is very good at math. He's not at all shy and is confident about learning new skills. ____
3. Hannah loves everything to do with fashion. She knows what makes people look great and what doesn't, and isn't afraid to tell them! She enjoys learning, too. ____
4. Marcus is very sociable; he's good at talking and gets along well with all kinds of people. He's also very honest and can usually tell if someone is lying. ____
5. Ray has excellent speaking and writing skills. He always did well in school and wants to study hard in college. He hates making mistakes! ____

HOME BLOG PODCASTS ABOUT CONTACT

Guest blogger Marc writes about seven interesting careers.

Find the right career for you

A To be successful, you must be passionate about the truth. You'll need the confidence to ask people difficult questions. You may need to make yourself unpopular with important people. And, of course, you'll need to have excellent writing skills, as well as to be able to communicate clearly.

B This is a very creative job, so you need good drawing skills. However, you should be able to see your clothes in your head *before* you put your pencil to paper. But loving clothes and being good at art isn't enough. It's a competitive business and you need to understand your markets and be able to calculate the cost of materials, etc.

C This will only suit you if you're someone who pays attention to detail. Your work must be absolutely accurate. You also need good time-management skills: financial information is extremely important for a business and must be available at the right time. Many top people in this job are senior managers, so if you do well, you might be promoted quickly.

D You're often the first person a customer meets when they visit a company or a hotel, so you must look smart and communicate in a friendly, professional way. You might have to deal with difficult or rude people, so you need to be calm and polite. You don't need a lot of qualifications, but you will need to use your firm's computer and phone systems.

E If you think you'll be good at this, don't do it! You need to be *great*, not good! The best people are extremely confident and excellent communicators, but that doesn't mean talking all the time. You need to listen, too. Above all, you need to know when it's worth pushing, and when to walk away.

F For such a competitive career, you'll need excellent grades to be able to get a degree. You'll need to analyze information quickly and accurately. And using language effectively is essential for understanding technical documents and communicating with clients. You must be able to express yourself clearly and logically.

G This is a creative job—up to a point! Relationships are important, too, and you can earn respect by giving clients good advice. There's no point giving a perfect cut if it doesn't suit someone's face and features. You don't have to do particularly well in school, but you need great technical skills. The best professionals continue to take courses throughout their career.

UNIT 5

Mind and body

5A LANGUAGE

GRAMMAR: *should/shouldn't*

1 Match problems 1–8 with the best advice and circle *should* or *shouldn't* in a–h.

1 My car keeps breaking down. ____
2 I feel so tired all the time. ____
3 I'm extremely stressed at work. ____
4 I never have enough money to go on vacation. ____
5 I have a lot of problems with my teeth. ____
6 I'm bored with going to the same restaurant. ____
7 I sometimes feel very lonely. ____
8 I never get good grades on my homework. ____

a You *should / shouldn't* spend so much on clothes.
b You *should / shouldn't* ask your teacher's advice.
c You *should / shouldn't* stay up late.
d You *should / shouldn't* try the one that just opened.
e You *should / shouldn't* make some new friends.
f You *should / shouldn't* buy a better one.
g You *should / shouldn't* eat candy every day.
h You *should / shouldn't* speak to your boss.

2 Complete the sentences with *should* or *shouldn't* and the verbs in the box.

pay let feel give up ask visit apologize do

1 I couldn't believe how rude Paul was. You ____________ him speak to you like that!
2 I can't afford to pay my rent. What do you think I ____________?
3 We didn't do anything wrong, so we ____________ guilty.
4 It wasn't your fault, so I don't think you ____________.
5 Boris broke the chair, so I think he ____________ for a new one.
6 Your piano classes are going well. You definitely ____________!
7 My friend Beatriz is in the hospital. I ____________ her later.
8 Do you think Ryan ____________ Helen to go out with him?

VOCABULARY: Health and medicine

3 Choose the correct options to complete the sentences.

1 He had to carry a heavy box and now he has a _____.
a flu b backache c sore throat
2 I can't play tennis for weeks because my arm is _____.
a stressed b sore c broken
3 Feel Mila's face to see if she has _____.
a a temperature b a cold c an earache.
4 I have a painful _____, so I can only eat soup!
a headache b earache c sore throat
5 Felipe has a bad _____; we could hear it during the night.
a headache b cough c toothache
6 Charlie is _____ because he has too much work to do.
a stressed b sore c broken

4 Complete the words. The first letters are given.

1 I touched the hot oven and b____________my hand.
2 I have a t____________ so I'm going to see the dentist.
3 Don't play with that knife, Henry, or you'll c____________ yourself!
4 Daniel's daughter ate too much ice cream and got a sto____________.
5 The ball hit Luisa in the face and gave her a noseb____________.
6 He h____________ his leg badly and couldn't walk for days.

PRONUNCIATION: *should/shouldn't*

5 5.1 Listen to the sentences and write *should* or *shouldn't*. Listen, check, and repeat.

1 Do you think I ____________ tell Rob the news?
2 Gloria ____________ spend so much money on clothes.
3 You ____________ talk during class.
4 I agree that David ____________ get a new job.
5 Maybe Maria ____________ spend more time studying.
6 You really ____________ eat so much before exercising!
7 I don't think you ____________ worry about that.
8 He ____________ put less sugar in his coffee.

LISTENING: Listening in detail

1 5.2 Listen to Rebecca calling Joey on the phone. Are the sentences true (T) or false (F)?

1 Joey is Rebecca's brother. ____
2 Joey is at work. ____
3 Joey wasn't feeling well in June. ____
4 Rebecca tells Joey to see a doctor. ____
5 Joey doesn't have a job at the moment. ____
6 Rebecca wants to see Joey. ____

2 5.2 Listen again. Choose the best options to complete the sentences.

1 Rebecca thinks Joey is
  a at the doctor's.
  b in bed.
  c with his mother.
2 Rebecca's mother said that Joey had
  a a cough.
  b a sore throat.
  c a cough and a sore throat.
3 In Dallas, Rebecca tried to persuade Joey to
  a see a doctor.
  b get a different job.
  c work fewer hours.
4 Rebecca has a
  a cold.
  b cough.
  c sore throat.
5 Rebecca talks about
  a visiting Joey.
  b cooking a meal for Joey.
  c taking Joey to the doctor's.

3 5.3 Read these sentences from Rebecca's phone call. Mark the links between consonant sounds and vowel sounds. Listen again and check.

1 I suppose you're in bed taking a nap.
2 ... you're not feeling very well again.
3 She said you had a bad cough and a sore throat.
4 I'm just a little worried about your health.
5 You seemed a little stressed about work when we got together in Dallas.
6 I don't think that job is good for you.

4 Choose the correct verb collocations.

1 When do you usually *make* / *do* / *take* your homework?
2 *Make* / *Have* / *Take* a deep breath and try to relax.
3 If you *make* / *do* / *have* a mistake, draw a line through it.
4 When we *make* / *have* / *do* an argument, Sophie always wins!
5 It's a difficult exam, so just *make* / *do* / *take* your best.
6 We have to *make* / *do* / *have* a decision about where to go on vacation.
7 If you're tired, why don't you *take* / *have* / *do* a little nap?
8 Let's *make* / *take* / *have* a good talk over coffee.

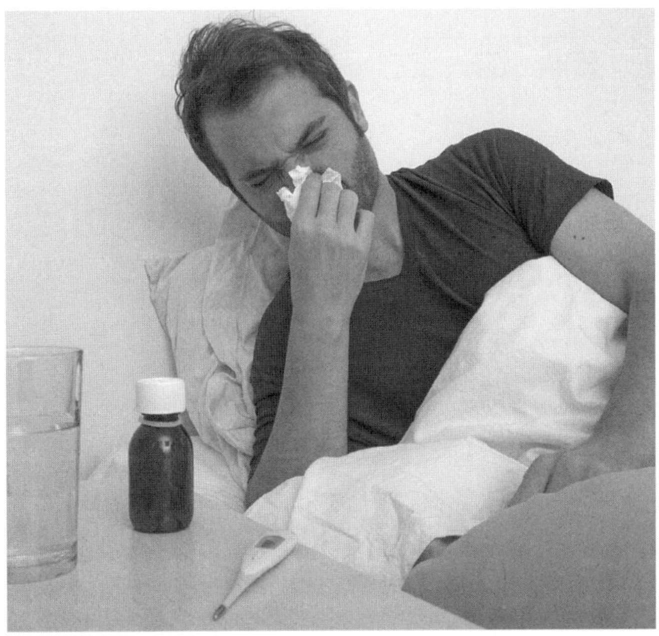

GRAMMAR: First conditional

1 Order the words to make first conditional sentences. Add commas where necessary.

1 the party / if / have / rains we'll / inside / it

_______________________________.

2 miss / the / you don't / hurry / bus if / you'll

_______________________________.

3 Luis I / can give / if I / the message / him / see

_______________________________.

4 have / problems just / if you / any / call me

_______________________________.

5 the movies / tired I / if / might not / I'm / go to

_______________________________.

6 be disappointed / if he / get the / there / job he'll / doesn't

_______________________________.

7 I have / from / call you / the airport if / enough time / I'll

_______________________________.

8 if Ellen / her I'll / be home / soon / I'll / calls tell

_______________________________.

2 Complete the first conditional sentences with the verbs in parentheses in the correct form.

1 If Mike ____________ (agree), we ____________ (go) on the subway.

2 We ____________ (not have) a picnic if the weather ____________ (not be) good.

3 Mom ____________ (be) angry if we ____________ (get) home late.

4 If you ____________ (not take) any medicine, you ____________ (not feel) better.

5 If the machine ____________ (stop), ____________ (press) this button.

6 I ____________ (call) you if I ____________ (need) a ride home.

7 Leonardo ____________ (be) upset if we ____________ (forget) his birthday.

8 You ____________ (hurt) yourself if you ____________ (not be) careful!

VOCABULARY: Emotions and feelings

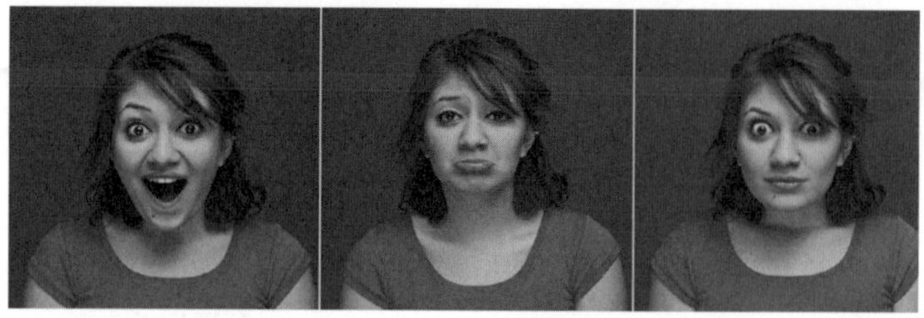

3 Match definitions 1–6 with adjectives a–f.

1 feeling worried about something ____
2 unhappy or sad ____
3 extremely happy about something ____
4 not worried or anxious ____
5 sad because you're alone ____
6 sure of your own abilities ____

a delighted
b confident
c calm
d nervous
e upset
f lonely

4 Complete the adjectives.

1 Her husband was very j____________ and didn't like her talking to other men.

2 Victor was p____________ of his new sneakers and showed them to all his friends.

3 You're very c____________ this morning! What's making you smile so much?

4 When I realized how badly I'd upset her, I felt g____________.

5 She was crying all the time and was extremely m____________.

6 I'm e____________ of your beautiful coat! I wish I had one.

PRONUNCIATION: *'ll* contraction

5 5.4 Listen to the sentences. Is *will* contracted? Circle the correct answer.

1 contracted / not contracted
2 contracted / not contracted
3 contracted / not contracted
4 contracted / not contracted
5 contracted / not contracted
6 contracted / not contracted
7 contracted / not contracted

WRITING: Writing an informal e-mail

1 Read Izzie's e-mail asking for advice about making friends. Number a–i in the order they appear. The first answer is given.

- **a** asking about the person you are writing to ____
- **b** mentioning a completely different subject ____
- **c** the ending ____
- **d** the reason for writing ____
- **e** the greeting ____
- **f** making an arrangement ____
- **g** the request for a response ____
- **h** the subject of the email __1__
- **i** the details of the problem ____

To: annabrown67@quickmail.com

RE: Advice, please!

Hi Anna!

How's it going? Hope you're enjoying your new job! Did I tell you I left home last month? I'm living in an amazing apartment in Antofagasta now.

That's why I'm writing. I'm having a really bad time, and I wanted to ask you for some advice.

My new apartment's big, and it's nice, but I'm very lonely! I'm a little shy (as you know!), so I'm finding it hard to make new friends. I miss my family so much now that I don't see them very often, especially my mom (I know, I'm such a baby!).

What do you think I should do? How did you make friends when you left home? And when will I stop feeling so bad?!

Anyway, the good news is that my brother's getting married in June! I'm really looking forward to the wedding.

Do you feel like going out for a pizza the next time I'm home, if you aren't too busy? There's a new pizza restaurant. It's kind of expensive, but not too bad. Let me know!

See you later,

Izzie, x

2 Write the contracted forms of these verbs. Which six are in Izzie's e-mail?

1. you are ________
2. she has ________
3. I am ________
4. it is ________
5. they have ________
6. do not ________
7. there is ________
8. did not ________
9. are not ________

3 Complete the sentences with *extremely, not very, very,* or *a little*. Use each one once.

1. I want to get more exercise but I'm a ________ nervous about going to a gym.
2. It's ________ healthy to eat so much junk food.
3. My friend goes running every day, so she's in ________ good shape.
4. These dance classes are ________ easy Anyone can take them.

4 Read the problem below, then write an e-mail to a friend, asking for their advice.

Your doctor says you are very unhealthy.

You need to get in shape and improve your diet, but you don't know how to.

You don't play any sports and you love pizza and ice cream.

- Structure the e-mail with a subject, greeting, reason for writing, details, request for response and an ending.
- Use contractions like *I'm* and *don't*.
- Use informal words like *Hi, How's it going?* and *anyway*.
- Use modifiers like *extremely* and *a little* to make adjectives and adverbs stronger or weaker.

Learning Curve

HOME BLOG PODCASTS ABOUT CONTACT

Tom and Sam talk about dealing with headaches.

LISTENING

1 5.5 Listen to the podcast. Does the speaker say these things? Circle *Yes* or *No*.

1	Headaches are the most common health problem in the U.S.	Yes	No
2	Tension headaches are ones that most people get occasionally.	Yes	No
3	Many headaches are caused by people's lifestyles.	Yes	No
4	Sleeping too much can cause headaches.	Yes	No
5	Yoga may help to prevent headaches.	Yes	No

2 5.5 Listen again. Complete the sentences with a maximum of three words.

1. In the U.S., more than ____________________ people have headaches regularly.
2. Bad headaches can make work or functioning in your ____________________ life difficult.
3. You should see a doctor if you have other symptoms such as a high ____________________.
4. Tension headaches last for about ____________________.
5. You can treat most headaches with ____________________ from the pharmacy.
6. The doctor advises drinking ____________________ glasses of water daily.
7. It's a good idea to sleep ____________________ hours every night.
8. Too much work or studying can cause ____________________, which leads to headaches.

READING

1 Read the blog about how to live to be 100. Match headings A–D with paragraphs 1–4.

A A difficult choice ____

B Don't forget to brush your teeth! ____

C Look at the data ____

D Healthy mind, healthy body ____

2 Choose the correct options to complete the sentences.

1. *Most* / *Few* / *Hardly any* people born after 2000 will live to 100.
2. From 1900–2000 life expectancy increased *more than* / *less than* / *the same amount as* in previous centuries.
3. People born before 2000 *can* / *can't* / *are likely to* live to be 100.
4. *All* / *Some* / *None* of the men who took part in the Swedish study were slim and active.
5. To live a long life, it's important to *take medicine* / *have children* / *enjoy yourself*.
6. If your father lives to 100, you are *more likely* / *less likely* / *about as likely* to live to 100 yourself.
7. For a long life, it *is better* / *is worse* / *makes no difference* if you have a young mother.
8. A woman who has a child after 44 has *more chance* / *less chance* / *about the same chance* of dying young compared to a woman who has children when she's younger.
9. To live to 100, what's best for the child is *the same as* / *different from* / *more important than* what's best for the mother.
10. People with poor teeth are likely to die *before* / *later than* / *at the same time as* people with healthy teeth.

HOME BLOG PODCASTS ABOUT CONTACT

Guest blogger Taylor explains how to live longer.

How to get to 100 ... *and beyond!*

The great news for anyone born after the year 2000 is that they're likely to live to be 100. In fact, life expectancy went up by 30 years between 1900 and 2000–the fastest increase ever! But people born before 2000 shouldn't be too jealous since many scientists say it's possible for them to live longer, too. But health advice seems to change from year to year, so how do we know what we should do if we want to live to 100?

1 Scientists in Sweden followed the lives of 855 men, all born before 1931. Ten of them lived to 100, and they all had certain things in common: they were slim and active, they exercised, they didn't smoke, and they kept themselves busy and cheerful.

2 It seems that if we want to live a long life, we should make sure we have a good time! Research shows that having interests and a feeling of purpose in life often does more to keep us young than pills and medicines. And numerous studies have proven how important it is to have a circle of friends, so you definitely shouldn't spend too much time by yourself.

3 The Swedish study showed that men, whose moms lived into their 80s or 90s, were much more likely to live to an old age themselves. But interestingly, the age of their dads had little effect. Scientists from the University of Chicago found that having a young mom increases your chances of a long life because her eggs were still strong and healthy when she had you. On the other hand, getting pregnant naturally over the age of 44 is a good sign for a woman. According to research from the University of Utah, if you do that, you'll be significantly less likely to die young than a woman who has children at a younger age. If you're a woman, that's a tough decision to make!

4 That's what your parents always told you when you were a child, and it turns out to be very good advice! Scientists have discovered that the bacteria that grow in a dirty mouth can cause heart problems, which may even lead to early death. So, strange as it may seem, if you brush carefully, you can prevent heart attacks as well as a toothache!

UNIT
6 Risks and experiences

6A LANGUAGE

GRAMMAR: Present perfect with *ever* and *never*

1 Choose the correct options to complete the conversation.

Gabriela [1]*Have / Did* you ever been skiing, Juliana?
Juliana No, I [2]*didn't / haven't*, but I'd like to. How about you?
Gabriela Yes, I [3]*have been / went* once when I was in high school. I loved it.
Juliana Actually, my brother just [4]*gone / left* for Vail on a skiing trip. He'll be there until Saturday.
Gabriela Lucky him! [5]*Have / Has* he ever been there before?
Juliana Yes, he's [6]*went / been* there a few times, although this time he went with his girlfriend, and she's [7]*never / ever* tried skiing before.

2 Complete the conversations. Write one or two words in each space.

1 **A** ____________ you ____________ seen a tiger in the wild?
B Yes, I ____________ one in India last year; it was amazing!
2 **A** Have you ____________ been to New York?
B Yes, I ____________ there several times.
3 **A** Have you ever tried snowboarding?
B No, I have ____________ done that.
4 **A** ____________ Matt ever ____________ to Turkey?
B Yes, he went there last summer.
5 **A** Has your sister ever been engaged?
B No, she ____________.

VOCABULARY: Phrasal verbs

3 Match the two parts of the sentences.

1 Poor Belinda! Her car broke ____
2 I really want to find ____
3 He wants to get in shape and has decided to take up ____
4 Could you buy some coffee? We've run ____
5 It's very hot in here. Could you turn ____
6 I didn't know the word, so I looked it ____

a out who took my phone.
b on the air-conditioning, please?
c up in the dictionary.
d out of it.
e riding his bike in the evenings.
f down on the way to work.

4 Complete the phrasal verbs.

1 I'll borrow your jacket and **give** it ____________ on Saturday.
2 Should I **go** ____________ writing my essay or finish it later?
3 There should be plenty of gasoline; I **filled** ____________ the tank yesterday.
4 It started as a small project, but **turned** ____________ a huge job.
5 Could you help me **clean** ____________, please?
6 You need to **fill** ____________ this application form.
7 I'll be ready in a minute if you just **hold** ____________.
8 Felipe has **given** ____________ eating meat because of environmental reasons.
9 Shall we keep these magazines or **throw** them ____________?
10 I had to **take care** ____________ my younger brother while my parents were gone.

PRONUNCIATION: *-en* sound in past participles

5 6.1 Practice saying the sentences. Pay attention to the pronunciation of *-en*. Listen, check, and repeat.

1 I've never driv**en** in the snow.
2 Have you ever writt**en** a poem?
3 She's never giv**en** a speech before.
4 Has he ever spok**en** to her?
5 I've never forgott**en** my parents' birthdays.
6 We have never eat**en** at that café.
7 Have you chos**en** your dessert yet?
8 Has she tak**en** her driving test?

READING: Guessing the meaning of words from the context

The idea of speeding down the side of a volcano, while clinging with all your strength to a little piece of wood, might strike most of us as terrifying. But some people travel thousands of miles to do just that. Every year, huge groups of thrill-seekers travel to western Nicaragua's Cerro Negro mountain to take part in the new extreme sport of volcano boarding.

Participants, dressed from head to foot in protective clothing, reach speeds of 80 km. per hour on their specially adapted surfboards. They hike up one side of the volcano, take a training class, and then "surf" down the other side, after having paused to admire the spectacular view from the top. Some stand as they race down, surfer-style, while others sit. All agree that it's exhilarating, though not everyone who does it is in a hurry to repeat it.

"I've never experienced anything like it!" says Jamie White from London. "It's completely unique. But although it's great to be able to say I've done it, I'm in no rush to do it again! To steer, you hold onto a rope that's attached to the front of the board and pull it one way or the other, but I'm not sure I did it right because I ended up crashing into some rocks. You can slow yourself down by keeping your feet in contact with the ground as you go. But again, I didn't quite get the hang of it, and I reached a really scary speed on the way down!"

1 Read the article about a new sport. Are the sentences true (T), false (F), or isn't there enough information to decide (N)?

1 Nicaragua's Cerro Negro mountain is the only place to do this sport. ____
2 You can use an ordinary surfboard for this activity. ____
3 Volcano boarders have to walk up one side of the mountain. ____
4 Jamie White is anxious to take part in this sport again. ____
5 He hurt himself on the way down. ____
6 He was frightened by how fast he moved. ____

2 Find the words in bold in the text, then choose the correct definitions.

1 If someone is **clinging** to something, they are
a lying on it.
b sliding off it.
c holding it tightly.

2 Something that is **terrifying** is extremely
a frightening.
b exciting.
c strange.

3 A **thrill-seeker** is someone who likes
a doing exciting and dangerous activities.
b doing a lot of exercise.
c traveling to new places.

4 A **participant** is someone who
a has not done something before.
b trains people to do something.
c takes part in something.

5 If something is **spectacular**, it is
a amazing to look at.
b extremely dangerous.
c very unusual.

6 An activity that is **exhilarating** makes you feel
a stressed and worried.
b happy and excited.
c relaxed.

7 Something that is **unique** is
a different from anything else.
b exactly like something else.
c very ordinary.

8 To **steer** something is to
a make it go faster.
b make it go slower.
c control its direction.

9 If you **get the hang of** something, you
a learn how to do it.
b fail to do it well.
c start to learn how to do it.

3 Complete the sentences about volcano boarding with the linkers *and, also, as well,* and *too*.

1 He found volcano boarding very frightening and he ____________ found it difficult.
2 Participants experience the thrill of speed and get to see fantastic views, ____________.
3 The mountain side is very steep ____________ it's also extremely long.
4 People who take part wear special suits. They wear helmets ____________.
5 The side of the volcano is hot. It's very hard ____________.
6 It's a demanding sport ____________ it also requires a degree of training.

GRAMMAR: Second conditional

1 Choose the correct options to complete the sentences.

1 If you could live anywhere in the world, _____?
  a where would you live
  b where do you live
  c where will you live
2 You'd be less tired _____.
  a if you are going to bed earlier
  b if you went to bed earlier
  c if you go to bed earlier
3 If you spoke to Luis, _____.
  a you can explain the situation
  b you could explain the situation
  c you will be able to explain the situation
4 You would lose weight _____.
  a if you ate less
  b if you were eating less
  c if you eat less
5 If you had more money, _____?
  a what did you buy
  b what would you buy
  c what are you buying
6 If you left now, _____.
  a you could take the bus
  b you can take the bus
  c you will be able to take the bus
7 I would take the job _____.
  a if they offer it to me
  b if they are offering it to me
  c if they offered it to me

2 Complete the second conditional sentences with the verbs in parentheses in the correct order.

1 If Manuel ____________ to save enough money, he ____________ a new motorcycle. (buy, manage)
2 If I ____________ you, I ____________ Henry for advice. (be, ask)
3 If she ____________ more time, she ____________ a foreign language. (have, study)
4 Amanda ____________ better grades if she ____________ harder. (study, get)
5 If you ____________ closer to me, we ____________ each other more. (live, see)
6 If I ____________ rich, I ____________ my job. (give up, become)

VOCABULARY: The natural world

3 Order the letters to make words that match the definitions.

1 a small river MASTER ____________
2 animals and plants in their natural environment LIDWEFIL ____________
3 the land along the edge of the sea HERSO ____________
4 when it gets light in the morning SIRENUS ____________
5 a low area of land, often with a river through it LAYVEL ____________
6 a huge area of water, like the Atlantic NOACE ____________

4 Complete the words. The first letters are given.

1 Those w___ ___ ___ ___ are huge; they'd be great for surfing.
2 There are some fantastic underground c___ ___ ___ ___ that you can explore.
3 The r___ ___ ___ ___ of these trees go several meters deep.
4 There was a fantastic s___ ___ ___ ___ ___ this evening; the sky was pink and orange.
5 I picked some apples from the tree's lower b___ ___ ___ ___ ___ ___ ___.
6 From his room he could see the mountain's snow-covered p___ ___ ___ s.

PRONUNCIATION: Sentence stress

5 6.2 Underline the words you think will be stressed. Listen, check, and repeat.

1 If I were you, I'd be annoyed.
2 She'd go back to college if she could afford it.
3 If you could play any instrument, what would it be?
4 If she was taller, she could be a model.
5 If Larissa came to the party, Alex would be happy.
6 I'd join you at the restaurant if I could leave work earlier.
7 Fatima would be happier if she had more friends.
8 If I didn't have to work, I'd go to the movies.

SPEAKING: Agreeing and disagreeing

1 6.3 Listen to Antonio and Carrie discussing vacation plans. Are the statements true (T) or false (F)?

1 Carrie likes Antonio's suggestions for what to do on vacation. _____
2 Antonio wants to do lots of different activities. _____
3 Antonio likes places that are popular with tourists. _____
4 They decide not to go on vacation together. _____

2 6.3 Listen again. Match phrases 1–8 with Antonio or Carrie's reasons for using them (a–h).

1 Absolutely! _____
2 I don't know. _____
3 Exactly! _____
4 Oh, come on! _____
5 I don't think so. _____
6 I suppose so. _____
7 I'm not sure about that. _____
8 You're right. _____

a Carrie doesn't want fresh air and exercise.
b Antonio admits that they are both tourists.
c Carrie agrees that they should decide on a vacation.
d Antonio agrees with Carrie's suggestion for a vacation.
e Carrie disagrees that being alone would be good.
f Carrie isn't crazy about going on a physically active vacation.
g Antonio prefers not to have Wi-Fi or comfortable beds.
h Antonio doesn't want to stay in a comfortable hotel.

3 6.4 Complete the phrases for taking turns. Listen again and check.

1 I want to do something exciting, something that's a physical challenge. What _______________?
2 Sorry, Antonio, you _______________ ...
3 It would be nice to get away from the rest of the world, _______________ think so?
4 Go _______________, Carrie.

4 6.5 Read the opinions. Then listen and respond using the phrases from exercise 2 and your own reasons.

1 It's best to go on vacation by yourself because you're more likely to meet interesting people.
2 Everyone should travel as much as possible. You can't understand the world if you haven't seen it!
3 Sports like sailing and mountain climbing aren't dangerous if you use the right equipment.
4 All students should take a year off from studying to go traveling.

Learning Curve

HOME BLOG PODCASTS ABOUT CONTACT

Tom and Sam talk about survival courses.

LISTENING

1 6.6 Listen to the podcast. Number these things 1–5 in the order the speaker mentions them.

- **a** how to find drinking water ____
- **b** figuring out where you are ____
- **c** the kind of people who take survival courses ____
- **d** how to create smoke signals ____
- **e** how to make a fire ____

2 6.6 Listen again. Choose the correct options to complete the sentences.

1 Sofia's course taught people how to
- **a** become a soldier.
- **b** survive in the wild.
- **c** deal with danger in Canada.

2 Sofia took the course because she
- **a** knew someone whose plane had crashed.
- **b** wanted to meet people with different jobs.
- **c** wanted to learn skills for dangerous situations.

3 The most important thing Sofia learned was how to
- **a** get water to drink.
- **b** find food in the wild.
- **c** make a shelter.

4 Sofia doesn't want to hunt animals because
- **a** it's too difficult.
- **b** she doesn't eat meat.
- **c** they frighten her.

5 Sofia learned how to use the sun to
- **a** walk in a straight line.
- **b** cross rivers safely.
- **c** see where she was walking.

6 Sofia learned how to get help by
- **a** being prepared.
- **b** waving to people.
- **c** lighting a fire.

READING

1 Read the blog about traveling alone. Check (✓) the things the writer talks about.

- **a** safety advice for women ____
- **b** the laws in different countries ____
- **c** choosing the best restaurants ____
- **d** finding the cheapest flights ____
- **e** organizing accommodations ____
- **f** meeting the local people ____

2 Are the statements true (T) or false (F), according to the blog?

1. Other travelers can often give you useful tips. ____
2. The writer had an enjoyable vacation traveling around Turkey. ____
3. When traveling with friends, you sometimes have to do things you don't enjoy. ____
4. It's good to be able to change your mind about what you want to do on a vacation. ____
5. Women are always in more danger than men when traveling alone. ____
6. Drinks are usually more expensive in other countries. ____
7. It's sometimes better to find out about a country when you arrive, not before. ____
8. People who try traveling by themselves may find they prefer it. ____

HOME BLOG PODCASTS ABOUT CONTACT

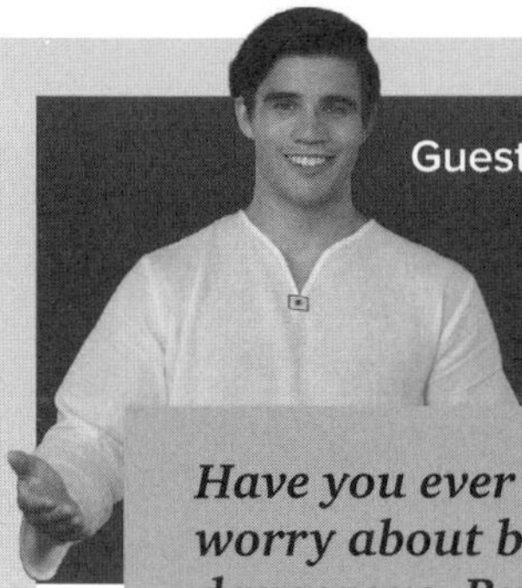

Guest blogger Ethan gives some tips on traveling by yourself.

Vacationing alone

Have you ever taken a vacation alone? For many people, it's a terrifying thought. They worry about being lonely, that accommodations will cost more, and that it might be dangerous. But it doesn't have to be that way!

If you go with a friend, you'll probably spend the whole time talking to him/her, but if you go by yourself, you're more likely to meet local people. Some of my most sociable trips have been to places without many tourists. Talk to taxi drivers, waiters, store owners; you'll get a lot of advice you can't find in the guidebooks! On the whole, people are remarkably friendly and generous. One of the best trips I've ever taken was to a remote area of Turkey, where several people invited me for meals in their own homes.

And just imagine, no more boring art galleries when you'd rather be white-water rafting, instead. And no more hanging around stores while your friend tries on fifteen different hats. Or if you just feel like spending the day under a tree with a book, there's nobody to complain!

It's worth giving yourself the flexibility to change your mind. If you plan everything before you go, you can end up missing out on unexpected opportunities. You might get an invitation to somewhere wonderful, or you might decide you love a place and don't want to move on. But if you know you're going to arrive somewhere late in the evening, make sure you reserve a hotel in advance. You don't want to be wandering around strange streets at night with nowhere to go.

And what about women travelers? Well, they can and do have equally good experiences as men. That doesn't mean there aren't some risks. Obviously you shouldn't get in a car with someone you've just met, for example, but that's just common sense, isn't it? It's worth putting the number for the police on your phone. And be careful in cafés and bars to make sure nobody puts anything in your drink. Some unlucky travelers have woken up several hours later with no money or passport.

Finally, do your research before you go. Find out about the local culture and social attitudes. How should you dress to avoid negative attention? Are there any typical tricks that thieves use on tourists?

So should we all be brave and try it? I definitely think so. The only danger I can see is that you may never want to go on vacation with your friends or family again!

UNIT 7

City living

7A LANGUAGE

GRAMMAR: Present perfect with *yet* and *already*

1 Order the words to make sentences. There may be more than one correct answer.

1 the / for / already / I've / tickets / paid

_______________________________________.

2 you / have / finished / essay / yet / your

_______________________________________?

3 it's / I've / 7 a.m. and / the house / cleaned / already

_______________________________________.

4 already / spoken / the phone / I've / to Carolina on

_______________________________________.

5 dinner / you / had / have / your / yet

_______________________________________?

6 gotten / home / she / from work / hasn't / yet

_______________________________________.

7 already / done it / have to / you don't / go shopping / because I've

_______________________________________.

8 you / Pedro's girlfriend / yet / met / have

_______________________________________?

2 Complete the sentences with the verbs in the box. Use the present perfect or simple past and the words in parentheses. There is one verb you don't need.

eat not open spend not make not take (x2)

1 The bread's not ready. I ________________ it out of the oven. (yet)

2 I was going to have some chocolate, but you've ________________ it. (already)

3 Camila ________________ any friends at her new school ________________. (yet)

4 This morning I gave both children $20 and they ________________ it. (already)

5 I'm hot and sweaty because I ________________ a shower ________________. (yet)

6 They built the new sports stadium, but they ________________ it ________________. (yet)

VOCABULARY: City features

3 Are the following sentences true (T) or false (F)?

1 You usually find bridges under the ground. ____

2 You can make statues out of stone. ____

3 Traffic lights control the movement of cars. ____

4 Fountains send water into the air. ____

5 Apartment buildings are always low buildings. ____

6 At an intersection, one street meets another. ____

4 Complete the words. The first letters are given.

1 In towns and cities, it's safer to walk on the s__ __ __ __ __ __ __.

2 You can cross the street at the c__ __ __ __ __ __ __ __ __.

3 Is there a t__ __ __ __ c__ __ I can put this empty bottle in?

4 The street was very dark because there were no s__ __ __ __ __ __ __ __ __ __ __.

5 We drove through a long t__ __ __ __ __ under the river.

6 Let's sit on this b__ __ __ __ to eat our sandwiches.

PRONUNCIATION: *just* and *yet*

5 7.1 Listen to the sentences. Which sound do the underlined words start with? Write numbers 1–7 in the correct columns. Listen again and repeat.

/ǰ/	/y/
___ ___ ___ ___	___ ___ ___ ___

1 Is Alfonso here <u>yet</u>?

2 Have you already been to the <u>gym</u>?

3 <u>Just</u> leave it there!

4 Vini <u>usually</u> has dinner with us on Fridays.

5 He applied for a new <u>job</u>.

6 Hi! How are <u>you</u>?

7 They look so <u>young</u>!

LISTENING: Listening for facts and figures

1 Read the sentences from the audio about bike riding. What type of information is missing? Match the blanks with a–f.

1 It's cheap, it's ____________ and, more than anything, it's fast. ____
2 Of course, I love to walk, too, but if I go anywhere on foot, it ____________ too long. ____
3 There are only about ____________ people living here. ____
4 I can ride my bike from one end of town to the other in ____________. ____
5 If I drive to work at ____________ in the morning, it takes me half an hour. ____
6 If I ride my bike, I can get to the office at ____________. ____
7 When I arrive somewhere, I don't have to look for a ____________. ____
8 All in all, I probably ride my bike for about ____________ a week. ____

a time
b verb
c noun
d adjective
e duration of time
f number

2 7.2 Listen and fill in the blanks in exercise 1.

3 7.3 Look at the example. Listen to these sentences. Mark where the /t/ sound links with the next word and where it is not pronounced.

1 Matt‿and I have already walk(ed) ten miles!
2 Bret went to Bermuda on vacation.
3 She missed the bus so she went on the train instead.
4 I don't eat meat!
5 He picked up his bag and crossed the street.

4 Order the letters to make words to complete the sentences.

1 He drove around the parking lot twice, trying to find a KRAGNIP CASPE ____________.
2 We stood on the FLAMTROP ____________, waiting for the train to arrive.
3 If we RTAST TOU ____________ at nine o'clock, we should arrive at noon.
4 I'm driving to Maria's house, so I could give you a FILT ____________.
5 I usually ride my bike there. It takes too long to go NO TOFO ____________.
6 We were stuck in a RACFFIT MAJ ____________ for almost an hour.
7 My favorite form of BUPCLI PARTNORTSANOT ____________ is the bus.
8 HURS HURO ____________ starts just before seven every morning.
9 The train was full of MOCMETURS ____________ on their way to work.
10 If we leave now, we should get there NO MEIT ____________.

GRAMMAR: Present perfect with *for* and *since*

1 Complete the sentences with *for* or *since*.

1 We've known Maria ____________ over ten years.
2 I've been a member of this gym ____________ 2014.
3 My parents haven't heard from Ben ____________ March.
4 Have you seen Jack ____________ you arrived?
5 I've been waiting here____________ ages!
6 Aline has been sick ____________ over three weeks now.
7 I haven't driven ____________ I passed my test.
8 They've lived in the same apartment ____________ years.
9 Pablo hasn't eaten meat ____________ he was a child.
10 Have you two known each other ____________ a long time?

2 Complete the questions and answers.

1 **A** How many years was she a teacher?
B She ____________a teacher ____________ three years.
2 **A** How long were you in the hospital?
B I ____________ there ____________ two months.
3 **A** How long ____________ Gabriela ____________ a vegetarian?
B For ten years.
4 **A** How many years ____________ you and Peter ____________ married?
B For nearly five.
5 **A** How long ____________ your father in the army?
B From 1990 to 2005.
6 **A** How long ____________ you study medicine?
B I studied ____________ eight years, until 2014.

3 Use the prompts to write questions and answers. Use the present perfect form of the verbs with *for* or *since*.

1 **A** how long/you/live/in Madrid
____________________________________?
B I/be/here/three years
____________________________________.
2 **A** how long/she/be/asleep
____________________________________?
B she/be/asleep/5:30
____________________________________.
3 **A** how long/Luis/have/a cough
____________________________________?
B he/have/it/the weekend
____________________________________.
4 **A** how long/your cousins/work/in France
____________________________________?
B they/work there/over ten months
____________________________________.

PRONUNCIATION: *for* and *since*

4 7.4 Practice saying the sentences. Are *for* and *since* stressed (S) or unstressed (U)? Listen, check, and repeat.

1 I've been here for three hours. S U
2 She's been sick since Wednesday. S U
3 We've known about it since noon. S U
4 Livia has lived in Paris for six months. S U
5 They haven't heard from her since April. S U
6 I haven't eaten since breakfast. S U
7 We haven't seen Maria for years. S U
8 She's been away since 2014. S U

WRITING: Writing an essay

1 Read Otto's essay and complete it with these linking words and phrases.

a The second reason **c** First
b In conclusion **d** Finally

Should cars be banned from the downtown area?

I live in a beautiful, historic city, but everyone agrees that there is a problem with traffic. Every day, over 60,000 people drive downtown to work or study, and pollution levels are rising. Our local council has suggested banning all cars from the downtown area. Personally, I think this is a very bad idea.

1 _____, how would people get to work? Houses in the city are very expensive, and people who live in the suburbs or outside the city already have long trips to work. In my opinion, it is unreasonable that they should have to wait for a bus to get downtown.

2 _____ is that I don't believe it's possible for everyone to use public transportation, walk, or ride their bikes to work. For example, people in wheelchairs need special vehicles, and many people have to carry heavy tools or equipment for their work.

3 _____, I'm worried that local stores and businesses will suffer. If people can't drive to the stores, they won't go at all. Most people don't want to carry bags full of shopping on a bus.

4 _____, I feel that banning cars from downtown is a bad idea. I would say that we should be looking at different ways of reducing pollution—ways that don't involve making life difficult for people! For example, we should develop better electric cars, improve public transportation, and make better bike lanes.

2 Find these phrases in Otto's essay. Then write sentences with your own ideas about whether or not cars should be banned from the downtown area.

1 Personally, ______________________.
2 In my opinion ______________________.
3 I don't believe that ______________________.
4 I'm worried that ______________________.
5 I would say that ______________________.

3 Use the words in the box to complete the arguments against Otto's opinion.

fresh air pollution healthier safe public transportation permission

1 In my opinion, banning cars would reduce __________.
2 I don't believe that it's __________ for cars and bicycles to share the streets.
3 I think that getting some __________ by walking or riding a bike to work is a good idea.
4 People who need to carry heavy equipment could get __________ from the council to drive.
5 Personally, I feel that people who can't walk or ride a bike should use __________.
6 I wouldn't say that riding a bike is difficult for most people, and it makes them __________.

4 Write an essay giving the opposite opinion to Otto's.

- Use ideas from exercise 3 or your own ideas.
- Organize your ideas into five paragraphs: introduction, reasons 1–3, conclusion.
- Give examples or evidence to support your opinion.
- Use some of the phrases from exercises 2 and 3.

Learning Curve

HOME BLOG PODCASTS ABOUT CONTACT

Tom and Sam talk about unusual ways to commute.

LISTENING

1 7.5 Listen to the podcast. What does the speaker say is the main advantage of how he commutes?

a It's a healthy way to get to work.
b His trip is quicker than other people's.
c He can still wear a suit when he's traveling.

2 7.5 Listen again. Complete the sentences with one or two words.

1 It takes Louie about ____________ to get to work.
2 He rides his skateboard on the ____________.
3 He has been skateboarding for ____________ years.
4 He thinks other people are ____________ of his trip to work.
5 He says the best thing about not using ____________ is not waiting for buses.
6 He thinks skateboarding is less ____________ than riding a bike.
7 He also uses his skateboard to go to ____________.

READING

1 Read the blog about car-free cities. Match 1–4 with paragraphs A–D.

1 places where little is being done to reduce the use of cars ____
2 how some cities have encouraged people not to drive ____
3 how technology can help people manage without cars ____
4 a new city where people won't need to drive ____

2 Are the sentences true (T), false (F), or is there not enough information to decide (N)?

1 People often need to drive to other places on their way to and from work. ____
2 Most people who work in cities drive to work. ____
3 In Milan, most people travel by public transportation once or twice a week. ____
4 London is a safe place to ride a bike to work. ____
5 In the new town near Chengdu, it will be easy for most people to walk everywhere. ____
6 Planners want people who work in Chengdu to drive there very quickly in their own cars. ____
7 It is easy for people in Helsinki to get information to help them travel without cars. ____
8 Most people in Helsinki already use public transportation. ____
9 Currently people in some U.S. cities prefer to ride their bikes around town. ____
10 In Sydney, town planning makes it easy for people to use cars rather than public transportation. ____

HOME BLOG PODCASTS ABOUT CONTACT

Guest blogger Penny writes about how cities are designed.

Car-free cities: dream or reality?

What's the number one thing you hate about cities? It's probably the traffic. Who wants to breathe in dirty air all day, or spend hours stuck in a traffic jam on their daily commute? On the other hand, we've had cars for over 100 years now and we rely on them, especially with our busy lives–rushing to drop the kids off at school before we go to work, or going to the supermarket on the way home. So how can town planners persuade us to leave our cars at home? Here are some different ideas from around the world.

A Since 2014, Milan has had a really interesting system: for every day residents leave their car at home, they get a voucher for the value of a ticket on the train or bus! And in Copenhagen, around half of all workers commute by bike on a huge, safe network of bike lanes. Perhaps London should try to do the same. Traffic there moves more slowly than the average bike rider, but the streets are far more dangerous on two wheels!

B In some countries, town planners working on new towns and cities are trying to reduce the use of cars to a bare minimum before they've even been built. For example, one new town in China, with a planned population of 80,000, is being designed so that all its stores, entertainment venues, work places, etc. are within a fifteen-minute walk from where residents live. And there'll be fast public transportation connections to the nearest big city of Chengdu.

C In Helsinki, local authorities are using phone apps to reduce car numbers. The city has several schemes for people to share the use of bikes and cars. The app allows anyone to quickly find the nearest shared bike, car, or taxi, or tells them the best and fastest bus or train route. Planners there hope that within ten years no one will need to drive in the city at all.

D Sadly, not all cities are encouraging car-free trips. It's true that 60% of people living in Paris don't own a car, but many U.S. towns and cities are designed specifically for the use of cars. And there aren't any alternatives yet. And in car-loving Sydney, things seem to be going backward. There are plans to get rid of pedestrian space to make room for even more cars!

UNIT 8

Food for thought

8A LANGUAGE

GRAMMAR: *Too, too many, too much,* and *(not) enough*

1 Match the pairs of sentences.

1 She needs a vacation. ____
2 I can't wear this sweater on a warm day. ____
3 She felt uncomfortable after the meal. ____
4 Can you open the window? ____
5 Let's turn the central heating on. ____
6 This coat's no good for winter. ____
7 She won't pass the exam. ____
8 She was hungry when she went to bed. ____

a She works too hard.
b It's too hot in here.
c It's not thick enough.
d She doesn't work hard enough.
e She didn't eat enough.
f It isn't warm enough in here.
g It's too thick.
h She ate too much.

2 Complete the conversation with *too, too many, too much,* or *(not) enough*.

A I'm so worried about my final grades. I haven't done [1]____________ work.

B I feel the same! I think I'm taking [2]____________ classes. I work late every evening, but then I'm [3]____________ tired to concentrate in class.

A I'm especially worried about French. Our teacher doesn't explain things clearly [4]____________, and he doesn't give us [5]____________ time to write things down.

B My problem is history. There's [6]____________ information to write and there's [7]____________ time. I want to study history in college, and if my exam results aren't good [8] ____________, I won't be able to.

A Well, try not to worry about it [9]____________!

B You're right. Getting [10]____________ stressed won't help!

VOCABULARY: Food and drink

3 Order the letters to complete the words.

1 s __ __ __ __ __ MONAL
2 e __ __ __ __ __ __ __ __ LPGAGNT
3 p __ __ __ __ CHAE
4 a __ __ __ __ p __ __ EPPL EI
5 p __ __ __ __ __ __ PPSREE
6 f __ __ __ __ j __ __ __ __ TIUR CIUE
7 p __ __ __ __ __ __ __ __ EAINLEPP
8 t __ __ __ __ __ s __ __ __ __ MOOTA UACE
9 c __ __ __ __ __ __ __ __ UUMCREB
10 s __ __ __ __ __ PRMIH

4 Complete the crossword puzzle. The first letters and total number of letters are given.

Across

4 meat from a sheep (4)
5 lots of people eat this for breakfast with milk (6)
8 a soft red fruit—you can make jam with it (10)
9 a fruit with a hard brown outside and a white part and liquid inside (7)
10 meat from a cow (4)

Down

1 a round fruit that is yellow and pink (5)
2 a vegetable with lots of green leaves; we usually cook it (7)
3 meat from a large bird (6)
6 a green salad vegetable (7)
7 we use this powder to make bread, cakes, etc. (5)

PRONUNCIATION: *too much sugar*

5 8.1 Look at the underlined words. Listen and circle the vowel sound that you hear. Listen, check, and repeat.

1 What should I do now?	/uː/	/ə/	/ʊ/
2 There aren't enough strawberries.	/uː/	/ə/	/ʊ/
3 I'm going to cook dinner.	/uː/	/ə/	/ʊ/
4 May I use your pen?	/uː/	/ə/	/ʊ/
5 Would you like a cup of coffee?	/uː/	/ə/	/ʊ/
6 I hate tomato soup!	/uː/	/ə/	/ʊ/
7 There wasn't any food left.	/uː/	/ə/	/ʊ/
8 You should put a jacket on.	/uː/	/ə/	/ʊ/

READING: Scanning for specific information

Food stories

ABOUT US RECIPES INGREDIENTS SHOP

Aquafaba ("Aqua what?!")

As regular readers of this blog will know, I know my food! I always say, give me a dish from pretty much anywhere in the world and, within two minutes, I'll tell you what's in it. However, this weekend, I discovered that maybe I don't know quite as much as I thought I did. A vegan friend of mine invited me over for dinner. (He turned vegan five years ago after seeing a really shocking movie on the dairy industry.) Just to remind you, vegans avoid all animal products, including honey. So I was expecting beans to be on the menu (and they were—lots of them—for the main course). But it was the dessert that took me by surprise—vegan ice cream. And how do you make ice cream, I hear you ask, without milk, cream or eggs? (I should say, how do you make nice, creamy ice cream without dairy products, because I've had some fairly unpleasant vegan ice creams in my time!) Well, it turns out that the key to good vegan ice cream, and a whole load of other desserts, is bean water. Yes, you read that correctly, bean water, i.e., the water that beans have been boiled in. (You know, the stuff you usually throw down the drain.) Bean water, my friend tells me, is called "aquafaba" by the vegan community. It's increasingly used to replace egg whites in savory and sweet vegan dishes, such as vegan butter, cheese, cookies, and cakes. And I can honestly say it works, although it does give the ice cream a slightly odd smell. It's so good, in fact, that the morning after my dinner date, I went straight to the supermarket for a can of beans. As I write, my first batch of aquafaba ice cream is firming up nicely in the freezer!

1 Underline the key words in these questions. Then scan the text about an unusual food and choose the best answer.

1 What did the blogger's friend invite her over for?
  a dessert
  b dinner
  c a dish containing eggs

2 What do vegans avoid eating?
  a milk and eggs
  b honey and cream
  c all animal products

3 What was the blogger expecting to be given to eat?
  a beans
  b vegan ice cream
  c a dessert

4 What, according to the blogger, is the key to many good vegan desserts?
  a beans
  b bean water
  c cream

5 In vegan cooking, aquafaba is used to replace
  a cream.
  b egg whites.
  c dairy products.

2 Look at the sentences. Are they true (T), false (F), or isn't there enough information to decide (N)?

1 The blogger is a vegetarian, not a vegan. ____
2 The blogger's vegan friend has never eaten animal products. ____
3 The main course of the meal included beans. ____
4 This was the first time the blogger had eaten vegan ice cream. ____
5 The blogger says that aquafaba is usually thrown away. ____
6 Aquafaba is much healthier than egg white. ____
7 She says the smell of this vegan ice cream is especially nice. ____
8 She has now tried making vegan ice cream with aquafaba herself. ____

3 Choose the correct linkers to complete the sentences. There may be more than one correct answer.

1 I liked the vegan ice cream, *however / but / although* I found the idea of bean water a little strange at first.
2 *Although / However / But* I'd tried lots of vegan ice creams, I'd never especially enjoyed them.
3 I don't have a recipe for the ice cream, *however / although / but* I'm going to follow my friend's instructions.
4 I usually know what's in a dish. *But / Although / However*, I have no idea what's in this.
5 I don't usually cook vegan food. *However / Although / But*, I feel inspired to try now.

GRAMMAR: *Have to, not have to,* and *can't*

1 Choose the correct options to complete the sentences.

1 You ____ finish that pie if you don't want it.
a don't have to b have to c can't

2 To pass this exam, you ____ get over 75% right.
a can't b don't have to c have to

3 You ____ talk to Peter because he has a lot of work to do.
a have to b don't have to c can't

4 This is Ben's medicine. He ____ take it three times a day.
a can't b have to c has to

5 Do we ____ bring our own food?
a can't b don't have to c have to

6 I have an important meeting. I ____ be late.
a don't have to b can't c have to

7 My new job is close to my house, so I ____ take the subway.
a can't b don't have to c have to

8 If you hear the fire alarm, you ____ leave the building immediately.
a don't have to b can't c have to

9 Why are you going home? Do you ____ get up early tomorrow?
a have to b don't have to c can't

10 It's Gina's birthday next week. I ____ forget to send her a card.
a don't have to b can't c have to

2 Complete the sentences with *can't*, or the correct form of (*not*) *have to*. There may be more than one correct answer.

1 We're going for a walk, but you ____________ come if you're too tired.

2 There are thieves in the area, so you ____________ make sure your car is locked.

3 Does Harry ____________ wear his uniform on the school trip?

4 We ____________ swim here; it's too dangerous.

5 Marta is very rich, so she ____________ work.

6 Larry is in a hurry because he ____________ leave in five minutes.

7 Do the children's parents ____________ sign these forms?

8 We can leave the classroom at any time. We ____________ ask for permission.

VOCABULARY: Adjectives to describe food

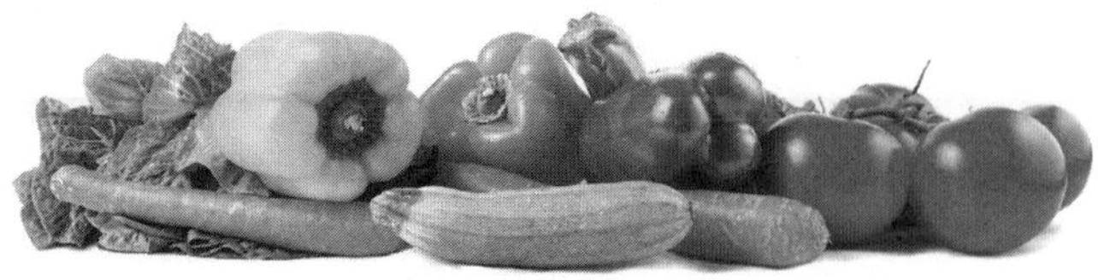

3 Complete the sentences with the adjectives in the box.

creamy salty sour healthy sweet crunchy bitter delicious

1 A ____________ diet should include plenty of fresh vegetables and fruit.

2 Alex is such a good cook. He made an absolutely ____________ curry last week.

3 You shouldn't eat too many ____________ foods like potato chips and olives.

4 Someone left the cookies out all night and they're not ____________ any more.

5 The coffee was much too strong and had a rather ____________ taste.

6 Maria loves ____________ foods like chocolate and cakes.

7 She served the apple pie with a lovely, ____________ sauce.

8 Add sugar to the lemon juice, otherwise it will taste too ____________.

4 Complete the adjectives. Some of the letters are given.

1 Laura put a lot of chilli peppers in the soup and it was too s___ ___ ___ ___.

2 Rob forgot to take the potatoes out of the oven and they were b___ ___ ___ ___ ___.

3 You haven't cooked this chicken long enough; it's still r___ ___ in the middle!

4 Paul loves un___ ___ ___ ___ ___ ___y foods like pizza and burgers.

5 You can make a t___ ___ ___y soup with chicken bones.

6 Does the restaurant use f___ ___ ___ ___ vegetables from their own garden?

7 Bean ice cream? It sounds d___ ___ ___ ___ ___ ___ing!

8 I don't eat meat. Are there any v___ ___ ___ ___ ___ ___ian dishes?

PRONUNCIATION: Sentence stress

5 8.2 Practice saying the sentences, putting the main stress on the underlined modal verb. Listen, check, and repeat.

1 You have to bring your passport with you.

2 Do we have to leave tomorrow morning?

3 She can't take the hotel towels to the beach.

4 You don't have to wait if you don't want to.

5 Parents can't help their children with this homework.

6 She has to arrive there before 9 a.m.

SPEAKING: Making and responding to invitations

1 8.3 Listen to the conversation between Karen and Brigit. Complete the phrases.

1 Do __________ trying out that new Japanese restaurant tonight?
2 I'm __________ I already have __________.
3 But would you be __________ the Japanese place another evening?
4 OK then, do you __________ go on Saturday instead?
5 Oh __________, I think __________ that evening.
6 Yeah. That would be __________, except I'll have to leave early.
7 Would __________ to stay over at my place?
8 That's __________ of you, thanks.

2 Are phrases 1–8 in exercise 1 used for inviting (I), accepting (A) or refusing (R)?

1 ___
2 ___
3 ___
4 ___
5 ___
6 ___
7 ___
8 ___

3 8.4 Listen to four people refusing invitations. Check (✓) the things each speaker does.

	Speaker 1	Speaker 2	Speaker 3	Speaker 4
Uses a pleasant intonation				
Apologizes before saying something negative				
Gives explanations				

4 8.5 Read the conversation then complete what B says. There is more than one possible answer for each blank. Then listen and say B's part aloud during the pauses.

A Would you be interested in going to the movies on Saturday? There's a new action movie that's supposed to be really good.
B 1 __________. My parents are having a party. It's been planned for a long time, and I can't miss it.
A Oh sure, I understand. The movie's playing all week though. Do you feel like going another night?
B 2 __________. I read an online review and it sounds really exciting. Sunday's good for me.
A Great. Would you like to come over to my place for a quick dinner before we go?
B 3 __________. Why don't I bring something for dessert?
A Excellent! See you then. Bye for now.

HOME BLOG PODCASTS ABOUT CONTACT

Learning Curve

Tom and Sam talk about healthy eating.

LISTENING

1 8.6 Listen to the podcast. Choose the best summary.

a Luca's diet is healthy now, but it wasn't when he was younger.
b Luca and his brother have unhealthy diets now.
c Luca's diet has always been very unhealthy.

2 8.6 Listen again. Are the sentences true (T) or false (F)?

1 Luca's mother still tells him to eat more fish. ____
2 When he was younger, Luca ate a lot of vegetables. ____
3 Luca didn't use to like green vegetables. ____
4 Luca's mother made him eat everything on his plate. ____
5 Luca's brother doesn't like vegetables. ____
6 Luca eats uncooked vegetables. ____
7 Luca avoids food with a lot of salt. ____
8 Luca eats unhealthy food while watching movies. ____
9 Luca really dislikes fish. ____
10 Luca's favorite sauces contain a lot of cream. ____

READING

1 Read the blog about cooking. What does it suggest?

a Everyone can learn to cook well with the right instructions.
b There are lots of things that can go wrong when cooking.
c You need lots of equipment in order to cook successfully.

2 Choose the correct options, according to the information in the blog.

1 What is the advantage of cooking a vegetable soup?
a It is healthy.
b It is easy.
c It is vegetarian.

2 Before you start cooking, what should you read?
a the first line of the recipe
b the first half of the recipe
c the whole recipe

3 Which of these things should you check before starting to cook?
a that you have the right equipment
b what time it is
c how many vegetables you need

4 What will a recipe <u>not</u> tell you?
a which vegetables to use
b what kind of knife you need
c exactly how to prepare an onion

5 What does the word *concentrate* in line 20 mean?
a to do something quickly
b to focus on one activity
c to be very careful

6 Why should you add stock to the soup?
a to make it smell nice
b to make it less hot
c to improve the taste

7 What does the last line of the blog suggest?
a You probably won't eat the soup.
b You will really enjoy the soup.
c You will definitely make the soup again.

HOME BLOG PODCASTS ABOUT CONTACT

Guest blogger Jack tells us how to stay calm in the kitchen.

Keep calm and go on cooking!

If you're new to cooking and want some basic tips, here's a great recipe for a simple, but delicious soup. I'll take you step by step through what to do and what not to do!

The first piece of advice is, always read the instructions to the end before you start cooking. You don't want to find out halfway through that you don't have all the ingredients (What if you've run out of noodles?), or some of the equipment (What if your neighbor doesn't own an ice cream maker either?), or enough time to cook it (Oh no, my girlfriend/boyfriend will be here in five minutes and all I have is a lot of raw vegetables!)

So, after you've read all the instructions, re-read the first line: "Peel and slice the onion." Take a sharp kitchen knife, and remove the first brown layer from the onion, and then the second (brownish) layer and then a third. Now, of course the recipe won't tell you when to stop and you don't want to end up with a really tiny onion. Make sure you have plenty of other vegetables: a red pepper, a couple of carrots, and a potato (even if slightly green). Chop them into small pieces (and don't worry about the green potato, no one will know once it's cooked).

Next, heat some oil in a pan. But how much oil? And what kind of pan? Pour in just enough to cover the bottom of a medium-sized saucepan. Then add the vegetables. At this point, whatever you do, concentrate! Do not attempt to do anything else! Do not answer your phone! Ignore the doorbell (unless it's the firefighters)! It's so easy to forget to keep an eye on things. Turn the heat down and let the vegetables cook gently for a few minutes. (Don't they smell good?) Then add a liter of water, plus two big spoons of stock (you know, that mysterious salty brown powder at the back of the cupboard. It may not look much, but without it, your soup won't taste ... anything like soup). Put a lid on the pan, and leave it for half an hour.

Of course, at this point, you'll forget the instruction not to answer your phone, and will end up talking to a friend for an hour. The final step (nearly) is to taste the "soup." And when you discover that even your dog won't eat it ... order takeout.
And that's why you should always read the instructions first!

UNIT 9

Money and shopping

9A LANGUAGE

GRAMMAR: *used to*

1 Complete the sentences with the words and phrases in the box. You will need to use two of them twice.

usually	use to	went	did	used to	go

1 David looks different now. He didn't ____________ have long hair.
2 On my sixth birthday, I ____________ horseback riding for the first time.
3 ____________ you use to visit your cousins when you were younger?
4 I used to ____________ to the park on Saturdays.
5 Yuri ____________ takes the bus to college.
6 She ate lots of ice cream as a child. She ____________ love it!
7 Did Daniel ____________ be so thin?
8 Lara doesn't ____________ go skiing in the summer.

2 Complete the sentences with the correct form of *used to* and the verb in parentheses.

1 I never ate olives as a child. I ________________ them. (hate)
2 Did Steve ________________ so hard-working when he was younger? (be)
3 She ________________ tennis in her teens, but doesn't now. (play)
4 My grandfather ________________ a cell phone. (not have)
5 Did your parents ________________ you bedtime stories? (read)
6 I ________________ bright colors in the past. (not wear)
7 Did you ________________ the train to New York? (take)
8 Alice ________________ so much before she went to college. (not go out)

VOCABULARY: Money verbs

3 Order the letters to make money verbs.

1 We aren't rich. We can't **fardof** ____________ to stay in that hotel.
2 This café's so expensive. They **ceragh** ____________ $10 for a cup of coffee!
3 She has a good job and **searn** ____________ more than her husband.
4 Don't forget to **apy kabc** ____________ the money Daniel gave you.
5 Jack's going shopping because he **tog apid** ____________ yesterday.
6 Don't **awest** ____________ your salary on things that you don't need!

4 Complete the sentences with money verbs in the correct form.

1 Can I ____________ some money to buy a ticket to the concert, please?
2 How much did you ____________ on that new jacket?
3 I ____________ my best friend $10 yesterday to buy lunch.
4 Their house is huge. It must be ____________ a fortune.
5 Which ____________ more, the blue shirt or the green one?
6 I'm trying to ____________ a little money each month to buy a new car.

PRONUNCIATION: *used to/use to*

5 9.1 Practice saying the sentences. Pay attention to *used to* and *use to*. Listen, check, and repeat.

1 She didn't use to play tennis.
2 They used to love going to festivals.
3 Did you use to walk to school together?
4 We used to work out at the same gym.
5 He didn't use to like classical music.
6 I remember that you used to enjoy dancing.

LISTENING: Identifying attitude and opinion

1 9.2 Listen to Tom and Natalie talking about shopping. Are these sentences true (T) or false (F)?

1 Tom likes to shop online. ____
2 Natalie prefers online shopping. ____
3 Tom thinks online shopping is easy. ____
4 Natalie doesn't like department stores. ____

2 Are the underlined phrases from the conversation opinion (A), feeling (B), or attitude (C)?

1 Yeah, I do most of my shopping online. I much prefer it. ____
2 Sure, you see it's so convenient to shop online. ____
3 I mean, to be honest, shopping for clothes online is the opposite of convenient. ____
4 I wouldn't say that's a big problem. ____
5 I get really fed up waiting! ____
6 I guess I just like stores, especially department stores. ____
7 I enjoy wandering from the clothes section to kitchen appliances. ____
8 I just remember the crowds and the lines: it was really boring! ____

3 9.2 Listen again and number the fillers 1–8 in the order you hear them.

a like ____
b I mean ____
c kind of ____
d Uh ____
e Well ____
f you see ____
g sort of ____
h So ____

4 9.2 Listen again and complete these sentences and phrases with fillers from exercise 3.

1 Sure, ____________, it's so convenient.
2 ____________, you just return it, don't you?
3 It's ____________ convenient because you don't have to leave your home.
4 You can ____________ get everything you want under one roof.
5 And, ____________, you can pick things up and see them and feel them.

5 Complete the sentences with shopping words.

1 That jacket was only thirty dollars? Wow! That's an absolute b___ ___ ___ ___ ___ ___!
2 I bought this bag on s___ ___ ___ for half the usual price!
3 Students get a 20% d___ ___ ___ ___ ___ ___ ___ in all our stores.
4 The pants didn't fit, so I sent them back and got a r___ ___ ___ ___ ___.
5 I asked the salesperson if I could e___ ___ ___ ___ ___ ___ ___ the jacket for a larger size.
6 Are you paying with cash or by c___ ___ ___ ___ ___ card?
7 I need to try this suit on. Where's the nearest d___ ___ ___ ___ ___ ___ ___ room?
8 Sometimes I used to go w___ ___ ___ ___ ___ shopping with no money in my pocket. I just looked at all the beautiful things.
9 There was such a long l___ ___ ___ to pay that I decided not to wait.
10 I paid for the items and the cashier gave me a r___ ___ ___ ___ ___ ___.

GRAMMAR: The passive

1 Choose the correct options to complete the sentences.

1 The wallet was _____ yesterday by a member of the public.
a turn in b turned in c to turn in

2 This park _____ by many people.
a isn't used b isn't using c doesn't use

3 When was the problem _____?
a discovering b discovered c discover

4 In the summer, dinner _____ on the terrace.
a served b is served c serving

5 A number of mistakes _____ during the investigation.
a was made b made c were made

6 Over 300 people _____ to the party.
a were invited b invited c was invited

2 Complete the text about the history of money. Use the present or past passive form of the verbs in parentheses.

It [1] __________________ (say) by many people today that "money makes the world go around." It's certainly hard to imagine life without it, but money [2] __________________ (not invent) until several thousand years ago in China. Tiny models of weapons and tools [3] __________________ (use) there as money. Before that, full-size tools and weapons [4] __________________ (exchange) for goods and services in a system called "barter." The first coins [5] __________________ (produce) 2,500 years ago in Lydia, in what is now Turkey. They [6] __________________ (make) from "electrum," a mixture of gold and silver. The first paper bills [7] __________________ (print) by the Chinese at around the same time. Fast forward in time, and today most goods and services [8] __________________ (buy) with credit and debit cards, or even using smartphone "wallets." Huge sums [9] __________________ (send) from bank to bank without anyone touching a single paper bill. Virtual currencies like Bitcoin [10] __________________ (accept) in some stores and online. Will bills and coins disappear completely during our lifetime?

3 Complete the sentences with the passive form of the verbs in the box. Use the tense in parentheses.

discover eat write invent
wash bake steal paint

1 The planet Uranus __________________ by Sir William Herschel in 1781. (simple past)
2 Bread __________________ every morning in our own bakery. (simple present)
3 I don't have a bike now. It __________________ last week from outside the school. (simple past)
4 The picture __________________ by Pablo Picasso in 1933. (simple past)
5 His car always looks perfect because it __________________ every week. (simple present)
6 This song __________________ by John Grant. (simple past)
7 Lunch __________________ in the main dining room. (simple present)
8 The first electric train __________________ by a German in 1879. (simple past)

PRONUNCIATION: Sentence stress

4 9.3 Underline the three words that you think will be stressed in each sentence. Listen, check, and repeat.

1 This soup is made with peppers.
2 The children are taught by their parents.
3 These plants are grown by my father.
4 The message was posted on Facebook.
5 Those houses were built in 1975.
6 That race was won by her cousin.

WRITING: Writing a formal e-mail

1 Read Elisabeth's e-mail complaining about a flat-screen TV she bought. Choose the correct words and phrases.

To: info@tvs2go.com

RE: Recent order (H23 100-A)

[1]*Dear Sir/Madam: / Hello,*

I am writing [2]*to tell you about / with regard to* the flat-screen TV that [3]*a man installed / was installed* in my house last Thursday.

First, [4]*someone delivered the TV / the TV was delivered* at 3 p.m., not at 10 a.m., as agreed. Second, as the man left, I noticed that some wires were hanging down at the back of the TV. When I [5]*pointed this out / told him about it*, he was extremely rude. Although he agreed to fix the wires, he [6]*did not / didn't* check to make sure the TV was working correctly.

[7]*I'm / I am* sure you will agree that this level of service is [8]*terrible / unacceptable*, and that a full refund of the delivery charge would be appropriate. Could you please arrange [9]*to pay the money / for the money to be paid* within a week?

I look forward to hearing from you soon.

[10]*Regards, / Bye for now,*

Elisabeth Miller

2 Match the correct options 1–10 from exercise 1 with these features of formal e-mails.

a full forms, not contractions ___ ___
b formal words and expressions ___ ___ ___
c passives to avoid being personal ___ ___ ___
d a formal greeting ___
e a formal ending ___

3 Complete the sentences with nouns made from these verbs.

refund argue increase deliver
improve discover discuss
decide organize inform

1 Last week I made the ___________ to purchase several items from your website.
2 The ___________ on your website was not correct.
3 I was not aware of the price ___________ when I ordered the product.
4 I was shocked by the ___________ that several parts were broken.
5 After a ___________ with one of your staff, I am still not satisfied.
6 I did not expect to become involved in an ___________ with one of your sales team.
7 Poor service will damage the reputation of your ___________.
8 Your company needs to make a big ___________ in the quality of its goods.
9 I will expect ___________ of a replacement within a week.
10 Please send me a___________ for the full amount of my order.

4 Write a formal e-mail complaining about a product you have bought recently.

- Include paragraphs giving the reason for writing, explaining the situation and saying what action you want taken.
- Remember to use the features in exercise 2.
- Use the sentences in exercise 3 for ideas.

Learning Curve

HOME BLOG PODCASTS ABOUT CONTACT

Tom and Sam talk about living with your parents.

LISTENING

1 9.4 Listen to the podcast. Check (✓) the correct statement.

a Sonia moved out of her parents' house because there were too many rules. ____

b Sonia's parents gave her money to help with her college tuition. ____

c Sonia went to live with her parents because she wasn't earning enough money. ____

d Sonia couldn't afford to go to college so she got a job instead. ____

2 9.4 Listen again. Complete the sentences with one or two words.

1 One of the ____________ in Sonia's life was when she graduated from college.

2 Sonia was scared that she might trip and ____________.

3 Sonia didn't know how she was going to ____________ her student loan.

4 Sonia owed a total of ____________ dollars.

5 It took Sonia ____________ to get a good job.

6 Sonia gave her parents money for ____________ and ____________.

7 When she was ____________, Sonia didn't like her parents' rules.

READING

1 Read the blog about money and relationships. Choose the best summary.

a Couples often break up because they can't agree about money. You should talk about money with your partner and, if you have very different attitudes, it's best not to get married.

b It's hard to change people's attitudes toward money, but if you understand how your partner feels, you won't feel so angry if he or she wastes money you wanted to save.

c Attitudes toward money are very important. You should try to understand how your partner feels and, if you have different attitudes, you should try to find ways to stop them from causing arguments.

2 Check (✓) the correct sentences, according to the information in the blog.

1 Things that happen in our lives can affect how we feel about money. ____

2 Attitudes toward money are more important than someone's personality. ____

3 People from poor families may not feel happy about borrowing money. ____

4 Attitudes toward money can change if a relationship lasts a long time. ____

5 Couples should be honest with each other when they talk about money. ____

6 We should discuss the emotional reasons why money is important to us. ____

7 People with very different attitudes toward money can't have a successful relationship. ____

8 Each person in a couple should pay the same amount of the bills. ____

9 Philip and Christa wanted to buy a home together. ____

10 When Philip saw Christa spending a lot of money, he thought their relationship wouldn't work. ____

HOME BLOG PODCASTS ABOUT CONTACT

Tom writes about money and relationships.

Money: how to stop it from ruining your relationship

Experts say that the main reason long-term couples break up is money—and the arguments it causes. Our attitudes toward money often come from our life experiences, and that makes them difficult to change. Someone brought up in a poor family may become very anxious about owing money, and be horrified at the idea of "wasting" it on things they don't think are necessary. So what can we do to stop money from ruining a relationship?

"We all have a money personality," says life coach Jo Handslip. "If we're thinking of a long-term relationship with someone, we need to get to know that side of them just as well as the other parts of their character. And whatever we may hope, we also need to understand that their money personality isn't likely to change."

The most important thing a couple can do is talk about money openly. "This isn't about money simply as a means of buying things," says Jo. "It's about what money represents to us." She says that couples should start by trying to identify what each of them associates with money, like success, security, independence, power, fun, or being free from stress.

Once they understand this, they can try to make their different attitudes work together. So, if one of you loves the freedom and excitement of spending money, and the other one wants the security of having savings, maybe you should agree to share the cost of bills, but keep the rest of your money separate. That way, the "spender" can only spend their own money, and the "saver" can feel secure. Or you could agree a maximum amount you can spend without asking your partner.

Philip Walker knows all about the problems money can cause. He and his girlfriend Christa broke up just two weeks before their wedding! "We were saving up for an apartment, so we agreed that the ceremony should be fairly small. But then I found out that instead of spending our savings on the wedding, Christa was going out to expensive nightclubs, celebrating with her friends, and buying lots of new clothes when she already had more than she needed. She'd buy the same dress or pairs of shoes in three different colors because she couldn't decide which she liked best! We ended up having a huge argument. In the end, seeing her throw our money away made me feel that she didn't see a future for us together.'

UNIT 10

Sports and fitness

10A LANGUAGE

GRAMMAR: Past perfect

1 Choose the correct tenses to complete the sentences.

1 That evening, I was tired because I _____ ten kilometers in the afternoon.
a had run b ran c was running
2 We _____ hungry because we'd already eaten.
a weren't being b hadn't been c weren't
3 By the time we arrived at the theater, the play_____.
a had already started b already started
c was already starting
4 When I met Lara I was sure I _____ her somewhere before.
a saw b was seeing c had seen
5 I'd put on a thick jacket and I _____ too warm later.
a was being b had been c was
6 I _____ how the movie would end because I had read the book.
a had known b knew c know
7 He had cut his finger while he _____ the meat.
a was preparing b preparing c had prepared
8 We arrived late to the party, so most of the food _____.
a was gone b went c was going
9 I didn't have any money with me; I _____ my wallet.
a forget b forgot c was forgetting
10 Camilla said she had met Igor while she _____ around Europe.
a traveled b was traveling c had traveled

2 Complete the sentences with the verb pairs. Write one simple past and one past perfect form in each sentence.

say / go   live / move   know / be   meet / know
pass / study   be / lose   finish / leave   be / leave

1 After we ____________ our dinner, we ____________ the restaurant.
2 The teacher ____________ angry because I ____________ my work at home.
3 He ____________ feeling stressed because he ____________ his phone.
4 Jorge ____________ all his exams because he ____________ hard all year.
5 I ____________ Javier once at Laura's house, so I ____________ who he was.
6 She ____________ in Italy for three years before she ____________ to France.
7 Eduardo ____________ most of the people at the club because he ____________ there before.
8 After I ____________ good night, I ____________ to bed.

VOCABULARY: Sports and competitions

3 Order the letters to make words that match the definitions.

1 to behave dishonestly in order to achieve something THEAC ____________
2 someone who watches people playing sports TRAPECOTS ____________
3 to win a point CROSE ____________
4 someone who practices a sport very well THELATE ____________
5 the person who controls the game FREEREE ____________
6 a prize for winning a competition HOTPRY ____________

4 Complete the words. Some of the letters are given.

1 She hopes to win a gold m___ ___ ___ ___ at the next Olympics.
2 Our team needs another goal to t___ ___ the score.
3 There was a huge c___ ___ ___ ___ watching last night's game.
4 Don't forget to w___ ___ ___ u___ before you go running.
5 Would you like to t___ ___ ___ p___ ___ ___ in our swimming competition?
6 You can't g___ ___ ___ u___ now. You're nearly at the finishing line!

PRONUNCIATION: *'d/hadn't*

5 10.1 Practice saying the sentences. Pay attention to the pronunciation of *'d* and *hadn't*. Listen, check, and repeat.

1 She'd already won the match.
2 He hadn't taken part in the competition.
3 We'd lost both games.
4 They certainly hadn't cheated.
5 We hadn't scored yet.
6 They'd tied in the semifinal.

READING: Finding information in a text

WEARABLE FITNESS DEVICES

News
Reviews
Fitness trackers
Watches
Forum

Fitness trackers

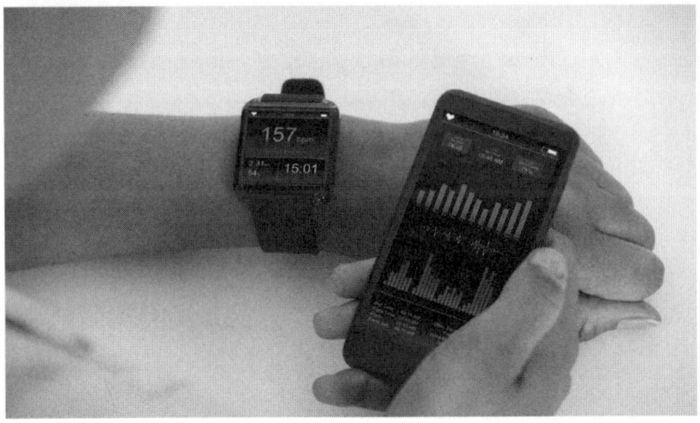

A Wearable fitness is everywhere you look. There are now hundreds of types of fitness trackers on the market, the simplest of which simply count the number of steps you take in a day. The more sophisticated models record your heartbeat, your food intake, your skin temperature, even how often you snore in your sleep! They allow you to observe and measure details about your own body that previously only doctors were able to see. Which, of course, is fascinating. But apart from providing interest in our lives, are these (often expensive) gadgets worth it? Do they serve any real purpose, other than making a nice profit for a number of companies?

B Well, it turns out that in a lot of cases they probably do. Not because fitness trackers provide 100% accurate data. (If you try out two different brands of fitness trackers, it's very likely that you'll get two very different step counts over the course of the day.) But because they're always there, often on your wrist, reminding you that you haven't moved or slept enough recently. Turn on your phone and a figure will pop up, telling you how well you're doing. (Some models will even tell you how well your friends are doing!) And that's just what most of us need, a constant reminder that we need to do better.

C And let's not forget that they're fun. Without a fitness tracker, we may know that we should use our legs more and our wheels less, but we may not actually do anything about it. When we wear a device that rewards us with a "ping" every time we reach our target step count, we are more likely to get off the bus two stops away from work and walk. Daily routines become a sort of game we play with ourselves, and who wouldn't that appeal to?

1 Read the text about gadgets that measure your fitness, then match paragraphs A–C with three of summaries 1–6.

1 A disadvantage of wearable fitness devices. ____
2 What do fitness trackers do? ____
3 The companies that make these fitness devices. ____
4 The enjoyment factor of wearable fitness devices. ____
5 The author's experience of these fitness devices. ____
6 Why wearable fitness devices are useful. ____

2 Read the questions and match them to paragraphs A–C. Then write short answers. There are two questions for each paragraph.

1 What part of the body do you wear some of these devices on? ____________
2 What do we all know we should do less of? ____________
3 How many different kinds of device are available? ____________
4 Where can you look at the information these devices collect? ____________
5 What activity do we know we should do more often? ____________
6 What can some devices count while you are in bed? ____________

3 Complete the sentences with *example*, *for*, *like*, or *such*.

1 We can all get more exercise, __________ instance, by walking rather than driving.
2 With this device daily routines, __________ going upstairs and walking home from the station, can be fun.
3 Everyone can now monitor aspects of their body's behavior, __________ as their heartbeat and temperature.
4 We can find out, for __________, how deeply we're sleeping.

GRAMMAR: Reported speech

1 Complete the sentences with *said* or *told*.

1 She ____________ she would call me on the weekend.
2 Nora and Lucia ____________ me they had seen you at the gym.
3 She ____________ me that Gabriel had gone to the meeting.
4 He ____________ that Yolanda would take Lola to the airport.
5 Isaac ____________ he would talk to Miguel about the problem.
6 He ____________ that Sophia liked her colleagues.
7 Paula ____________ me she had met you at the wedding.
8 He ____________ me that Lily wasn't coming.

2 Use the prompts to rewrite the sentences in reported speech.

1 "I'll call you from the station."
My sister / tell me / she call me / from the station
____.

2 "Dad can cook dinner for you and Laura."
My mom / say / Dad cook / dinner for us
____.

3 "I didn't see Luke in town on Saturday."
He / tell me / he / not see / Luke in town on Saturday
____.

4 "I just bought a new computer."
Maria / say / she buy / a new computer
____.

5 "We're going to move to France."
He / tell me / they going to move / to France
____.

6 "I haven't made up my mind."
She / say / she / not make up / her mind
____.

7 "I'm meeting David on Friday."
Victor / tell me / he meet David / on Friday
____.

8 "Alba loves going for walks."
He / say / Alba love / going for walks
____.

VOCABULARY: Parts of the body

3 Match parts of the body a–j with the definitions 1–8.

1 This is in your head and controls how you think. ____
2 This helps your arm bend. ____
3 These are the soft edges of the mouth. ____
4 This helps your leg bend. ____
5 This part of the body contains the heart. ____
6 This is the soft part of the front of the body, above your legs. ____
7 These are the two parts of your body at the tops of your arms. ____
8 This is just above your foot at the bottom of your leg. ____

a shoulders	**e** stomach	**i** elbow
b thumb	**f** lips	**j** knee
c chest	**g** forehead	
d brain	**h** ankle	

4 Complete the words. The first letters are given.

1 After running, the m___ ___ ___ ___ ___ ___ in my legs were tired.
2 She'd broken a b___ ___ ___ in her foot and couldn't walk.
3 Anna was wearing a pretty scarf around her n___ ___ ___.
4 A healthy diet and regular exercise are good for your h___ ___ ___ ___ .
5 He was wearing sandals, so I could see his t___ ___ ___.
6 After a few days in the sun, her s___ ___ ___ was really brown.
7 Why is she pointing a f___ ___ ___ ___ ___ at me?
8 Victor has an expensive-looking watch on his left w___ ___ ___ ___.

PRONUNCIATION: Unstressed *that*

5 10.2 Listen to the sentences. Is *that* strong (S) or weak (W)? Listen, check, and repeat.

1 Monica said that she was leaving. ____
2 Is that your cousin over there? ____
3 That's not what I said! ____
4 Kevin told me that I was wrong. ____
5 Pam said that the party started at eight. ____
6 Could you give me that book, please? ____
7 Beatriz told Clara that she was angry. ____
8 Sara likes the blue bike, but I like that one. ____

SPEAKING: Making inquiries

1 10.3 Gabriella is a guest at an expensive hotel. Listen to her conversation with the receptionist. Are the statements true (T) or false (F)?

1 Gabriella didn't know that the hotel had a fitness center. ____
2 The exercise room has a lot of equipment that guests can use. ____
3 Gabriella wants someone to show her the gym. ____
4 Guests don't have to pay to use the swimming pool. ____
5 The swimming pool closes at night. ____
6 The receptionist will send an extra towel to Gabriella's room. ____

2 10.3 Listen again. You will hear seven of these phrases. Write G (Gabriella) or R (receptionist).

a Can I help you? ____
b Could you give me some information about ..., please? ____
c Just one more thing. ____
d Excuse me, could you tell me ...? ____
e I'd also like to ask about ... ____
f Does that sound OK? ____
g I was told ... Is that true? ... ____
h Is there anything else... ? ____
i Should I ...? ____
j Can I just double check? Do you ...? ____
k Would you like me to ...? ____
l Could I speak to someone about ...? ____
m I was hoping you could help me. ____

3 Put the phrases from exercise 2 into the correct categories.

1 starting an inquiry politely ___ ___ ___ ___
2 asking for additional information ___ ___ ___ ___
3 being helpful ___ ___ ___ ___ ___

4 10.4 Use the phrases in exercise 2 to complete these conversations. There may be more than one possible answer. Then listen and say the missing part aloud.

1 In a sports store

A Good morning. Can I help you?
B Hello. [1] ____________ sneakers, please? I'm looking for a pair for long-distance running.
A Yes, we have several running shoes. Can I bring some for you to try on?
B That would be great, thanks. [2] ____________ waterproof jackets.
A We don't have any available at the moment, but here's a catalog. You can order them online. Does that sound OK?

2 At the gym

A Excuse me, can I take Pilates classes here?
B Yes, we have several teachers. [3] ____________ give you a list?
A Great, thanks.
B You can call them to arrange a time. [4] ____________?
A Yes, perfect, thanks.
B Here's the list. [5] ____________?
A No, that's everything. Thanks for your help.

Learning Curve

HOME BLOG PODCASTS ABOUT CONTACT

Tom and Sam talk about joining a gym.

LISTENING

1 10.5 Listen to the podcast. Check (✓) the parts of the body that are mentioned.

a foot ____
b neck ____
c muscle ____
d ankle ____
e wrist ____
f stomach ____
g shoulder ____
h bone ____
i heart ____
j knee ____

2 10.5 Listen again. Choose the correct options to complete the sentences.

1 How long has Harry been going to the sports center?
a about one year
b about two years
c about five years

2 For his height, Harry
a weighs too little.
b weighs the right amount.
c weighs too much.

3 Harry wants a workout that's good for his
a stomach.
b muscles.
c heart.

4 Harry says that he
a has always been active.
b has never done much exercise.
c has never injured himself.

5 Harry had to have an operation when he was
a eight.
b eleven.
c twenty.

6 What happened while Harry was skiing?
a He injured his leg.
b He damaged part of his arm.
c He caused a serious accident.

READING

1 Read the blog about sports injuries. Choose the best summary.

a Peter didn't prepare enough for his run and, because of his injury, he will never be able to run again.
b Peter hadn't realized there was a problem with his ankle and made things worse by doing more exercise.
c Peter wasn't used to doing much exercise, and hurt his ankle badly soon after starting his run.

2 Choose the correct options to complete the sentences.

1 According to Peter, after a sports injury you feel
a upset and annoyed.
b surprised and frightened.
c tired and embarrassed.

2 Peter hurt his ankle
a when he got up one day.
b while he was running.
c when he was preparing to run.

3 Peter's doctor told him
a to stop running for a few weeks.
b to run shorter distances.
c to stop running completely.

4 Peter had
a had a few injuries in the past.
b never injured himself before.
c only recently started running.

5 Peter says that stress
a makes it take longer to recover from injury.
b is hard for most people to control.
c can make it difficult for him to run.

6 Peter says that he
a thought his ankle would never get better.
b was impatient to recover as quickly as possible.
c did what his doctor had told him to do.

HOME BLOG PODCASTS ABOUT CONTACT

Guest blogger Kate gets some advice on recovering from sports injuries.

How I got back on track

We all know we should get plenty of exercise and many of us have a favorite sport or activity. But what happens if you suffer an injury and can't practice the sport you love? How do you cope with it, and how do you recover from it? Peter Jackson, sports coach and runner, told us about his experience of being injured.

"It's tough. You feel so many negative emotions. You're angry because you can't practice your sport. You feel disappointed because your body has failed you. And you're bored because you can't do what you want to do!

One morning last year I got up and noticed a problem with my right ankle. It was a slight pain at first and I thought it would go away. I'd done a long run the day before—a few miles more than usual—and thought maybe that was the reason. Anyway, I went running, as usual. I'd done everything correctly to prepare. I'd put a bandage on for support and, of course, I'd warmed up before starting.

But as I ran, the pain got worse and worse and, after three miles, I had to give up and go home. The next day, I saw my doctor who told me that I'd injured my ankle badly and that I would have to rest it for four to six weeks; that meant no running at all! It was kind of a shock. Until that point, I'd run every day for the previous four or five years, with no problems. Suddenly, I had to learn new habits. Most importantly, I had to start listening to my body and it was telling me to rest.

Of course, at first I felt very stressed by not being able to run, but I learned to manage that. It's often said that stress is caused by the feeling that we can't control a situation, and stress stops the body from getting better. So the first thing I had to understand was that I was in control because I was helping myself get better. I couldn't take part in running any more, but by resting my ankle and doing the exercises that the doctor had shown me, I was taking part in my recovery. I learned to be patient, to accept that it takes time to get better and, above all, I learned to be positive and to believe that I would recover.

UNIT
11 At home

11A LANGUAGE

GRAMMAR: *-ing*/infinitive verb patterns

1 Choose the correct options to complete the sentences.

1 I have arranged _____ Rita this evening.
  a meeting   b to meet
2 Did you finish _____ your bedroom yet?
  a decorating   b to decorate
3 Frankie can't stand _____ early.
  a getting up   b to get up
4 The company is planning _____ its factory in Ohio.
  a closing   b to close
5 Oh no! I forgot _____ my passport!
  a bringing   b to bring
6 Would you mind _____ dinner tonight?
  a cooking   b to cook
7 Gary hopes _____ a place on the team.
  a getting   b to get
8 Do you feel like _____ to the beach today?
  a going   b to go
9 I can't imagine _____ a marathon!
  a running   b to run
10 Unfortunately, I can't afford _____ a vacation this year.
  a taking   b to take

2 Complete the text with the correct form of the verbs in the box.

get move tell play
visit stay hang out pay

Last year, I decided [1]_____________ to another city. I was bored with my job, and I wanted a change. I'm the kind of person that hates [2]_____________ in the same place for too long. Luckily, I managed [3]_____________ a new job fairly quickly. My new company even offered [4]_____________ my rent for three months while I looked for a place to buy. The only problem was my great friend, Stan. He kept [5]_____________ me that I would be lonely and that I'd miss [6]_____________ with him and our other friends. I did feel sorry about leaving Stan, but I knew I'd make new friends quickly. I love [7]_____________ soccer and joining a team is always a good way to meet people. However, I promised [8]_____________ Stan as often as I could, and I've kept my promise.

VOCABULARY: Household items

3 Order the letters to make words that match the descriptions.

1 It keeps you warm in bed. FMCOETRRO _____________
2 You turn it on and water comes out. TFUACE _____________
3 You put dirty clothes in it. GASWNHI CHANMIE _____________
4 You keep your clothes in it. THESC FO REWARDS _____________
5 They are made of thin material and go on a bed. THESES _____________
6 It keeps your house warm. ANCTLER THIGANE _____________

4 Complete the crossword puzzle.

Across

3 Put the _____________ on the sofa.
5 I sleep best with a soft _____________ under my head.
8 Pia had a _____________ full of beautiful clothes.
9 I washed my hands in the bathroom _____________.

Down

1 A _____________ is a small carpet.
2 All the dirty dishes need to go in the _____________.
4 It was cold, so we put an extra _____________ on the bed.
6 Is the _____________ hot enough yet to do my shirt?
7 The cake must be done, so take it out of the _____________.

PRONUNCIATION: Sentence stress

5 11.1 Listen to these sentences and repeat them. Pay attention to the way *to* is pronounced.

1 Gary can't afford to buy a new laptop.
2 The children enjoy playing in the park.
3 We plan to meet our friends at eight.
4 I don't feel like going to the movies.
5 I forgot to lock the door.
6 Silvia doesn't want to come with us.

LISTENING: Understanding and interpreting information

1 ▶ 11.2 Read the sentences and look at the underlined words. Think about other words the speakers might use. Then listen to the conversation. Are the sentences True (T) or False (F)?

1 Johnny is extremely tired after doing the housework. ____
2 Johnny has cleaned the kitchen floor. ____
3 Marta says Johnny's roommates will be very pleased with him. ____
4 As part of Marta and Sara's agreement, Marta cleans the house. ____
5 Marta tells Johnny she hates cleaning. ____
6 Marta's roommate, Sara, really likes food. ____
7 Marta says the meals she cooks are very good. ____
8 Marta says she spends a lot of time deciding what to cook. ____

2 ▶ 11.2 Listen again and check and write the actual words the speakers use.

1 extremely tired ____________
2 cleaned ____________
3 very pleased ____________
4 agreement ____________
5 hates ____________
6 really likes ____________
7 very good ____________
8 a lot of time ____________

3 Read the short conversations. Write the words that the speakers don't say.

1 **A** She was angry.
B No, she wasn't. ____________
2 **A** Do you think Maria's happy at work?
B Not so sure about that! ____________
3 **A** What's wrong?
B Computer's not working! ____________
4 **A** You look really stressed.
B Yes! Big problem with the plans for Saturday! ____________
5 **A** Sara doesn't like cooking, I'm guessing?
B No, hates it! ____________

4 Match a–e with missing words 1–5 in exercise 3.

a pronouns ____
b articles ____
c *be* and auxiliary verbs ____
d *There is/are* ____
e avoid repeating words ____

5 Match the two parts of the sentences.

1 We'll need to set ____
2 Tom said he was mopping ____
3 Could you hang out ____
4 I completely forgot to water ____
5 After we finished eating, we loaded ____
6 Ella got up and had breakfast, then made ____
7 He dropped some food and had to vacuum ____
8 Don't forget to take out ____

a the plants in the garden.
b these clothes to dry, please?
c the trash, please.
d the carpet.
e the dishwasher.
f the bathroom floor when I called.
g her bed.
h the dinner table for six people.

GRAMMAR: Articles

1 Match the two parts of the sentences.

1 I would really love a ____
2 Paul said he would like an ____
3 I think I will enjoy the ____
4 We could have ____
5 Esther talked a lot about ____
6 Laura explained how ____
7 Rick told me about an ____
8 Maria described a ____

a book you told us about.
b to get to Bill's house.
c drink.
d village in China.
e old friend who was a musician.
f orange.
g politics.
h breakfast before we go.

2 Complete the sentences with the correct article or – (no article).

1 Vivian goes to the doctor's twice ____________ year.
2 We went to ____________ amazing concert last night.
3 I'm a little scared of ____________ dogs.
4 She gave ____________ taxi driver a big tip.
5 Patsy has to go to ____________ hospital tomorrow.
6 I usually have sandwiches for ____________ lunch.
7 ____________ Monday is the first day of the working week.
8 They have to go to ____________ bank before it closes.
9 What's ____________ name of Pete's girlfriend?
10 My sister is ____________ engineer.

3 Read the review and choose the correct sequence of articles, A, B, or C.

"Spectacles" review *****

This week we're reviewing Spectacles, [1]_____ pair of sunglasses that can take [2]_____ videos. [3]_____ product is made by [4]_____ video and messaging app, Snapchat. [5]_____ videos are [6]_____ unusual shape: they're round, similar to human vision. Spectacles' 10-second video clips are sent via Bluetooth to users' smartphones.

	1	2	3	4	5	6
A	1 –	2 –	3 –	4 the	5 –	6 a
B	1 a	2 –	3 The	4 the	5 The	6 an
C	1 a	2 the	3 The	4 –	5 The	6 the

VOCABULARY: Words to describe materials and clothes

4 Complete the sentences with the words in the box.

silk fur casual wood wool metal

1 I'm an animal lover, so I don't wear ____________ coats.
2 You need to polish ____________ jewelry to make it shine.
3 It's best to wash ____________ shirts by hand.
4 We gave Helga an unusual ____________ ring for her birthday.
5 In winter, I wear a ____________ sweater to keep warm.
6 Joe packed some ____________ clothes for his vacation.

5 Complete the words.

1 My sister is a vegetarian and won't even buy l___ ___ ___ ___ ___ ___ ___ shoes.
2 You should wear f___ ___ ___ ___ ___ clothes for an interview.
3 In summer Felipe prefers short-sleeved c___ ___ ___ ___ ___ ___ shirts.
4 We aren't allowed to wear d___ ___ ___ ___ jeans to work.
5 Are these pants too t___ ___ ___ ___? I think I need a larger size.
6 She didn't buy the skirt with flowers on it because she wanted something p___ ___ ___ ___.

PRONUNCIATION: *the*

6 11.3 Listen and circle the pronunciation of *the* that you hear. Listen, check, and repeat.

1 We need to take **the** early train.	/ðə/	/ði/
2 Where are all **the** other people?	/ðə/	/ði/
3 What time does **the** concert start?	/ðə/	/ði/
4 Should we meet at **the** usual place?	/ðə/	/ði/
5 Don't forget to bring **the** tickets.	/ðə/	/ði/
6 His house is painted pink on **the** outside.	/ðə/	/ði/
7 How did you do on **the** exam?	/ðə/	/ði/
8 I spilled juice on **the** carpet.	/ðə/	/ði/

WRITING: Making writing interesting

1 Read David's description of his friend's house and complete it with the words in the box.

so (x 2) because but although however and also as well

Michael's house

My friend Michael lives with his parents in a big modern house just outside the city. I think it's an excellent place to live [1]__________ it's really peaceful there, [2]__________ it's still easy to get to the city on the bus.

Michael's mom is an excellent gardener, and they have a gorgeous yard with lots of flowers. It [3]__________ has a large swimming pool, where we often hang out on the weekends.

[4]__________ the rooms in Michael's house are spacious, they're still very comfortable. In Michael's room, there's an old leather sofa [5]__________ lots of soft red velvet cushions. There's a lovely thick rug, [6]__________.

All the rooms have big windows [7]__________ they're bright and airy. [8]__________, most of them have thick, black blinds, [9]__________ you can make the rooms dark if you want to. That's especially useful in the living room, where we often watch movies.

2 Order the adjectives to complete the sentences.

1. He owns a(n) __________ bed. (huge/amazing/square)
2. Her bedroom has __________ curtains. (pale green/silk/fashionable)
3. My house contains a __________ living area. (spacious/modern)
4. Their home is full of __________ furniture. (old/oak/beautiful)
5. She uses __________ sheets on the beds. (Egyptian/white/cotton)
6. I don't like the __________ window frames. (horrible/plastic/modern)
7. On the table there is a __________ vase. (Chinese/large/round)
8. The dining room has a __________ carpet. (blue/gorgeous)

3 Find these words in the text and match them with synonyms a–d.

1	spacious ____	a	spend time
2	gorgeous ____	b	reach
3	hang out ____	c	large
4	get to	d	beautiful

4 Find two examples in the text of *where* and an example of what you can do there. Then complete 1–4 with your own ideas.

1. Greg's house has a gorgeous long yard, where __________.
2. Anna's cottage has an an old red living room, where __________.
3. Peter's apartment has an enormous square balcony, where __________.
4. There is a wonderful modern kitchen, where __________.

5 Write a description of a home you like.

- Use adjectives in the correct order.
- Use synonyms to avoid repeating words.
- Use linkers to give reasons and results (*so, because, that's why*), to contrast information (*but, although, however*) or add information (*and, also, too, as well*).
- Include a sentence with *where* and what you can do in a particular place.

Learning Curve

HOME BLOG PODCASTS ABOUT CONTACT

Tom and Sam talk about Tom's new apartment.

LISTENING

1 11.4 Listen to the podcast. Number these things in the order Tom mentions them.

- **a** closet ____
- **b** sofa ____
- **c** freezer ____
- **d** central heating ____
- **e** kitchen ____
- **f** comforter ____
- **g** refrigerator ____
- **h** chest of drawers ____

2 11.4 Listen again. Is each statement correct (Yes) or incorrect (No)?

	Yes	No
1 Tom has been in his new home for less than a month.	☐	☐
2 Tom moved in on the coldest day of the year.	☐	☐
3 Tom had to go to bed early to keep warm.	☐	☐
4 Tom was pleased the central heating was soon fixed.	☐	☐
5 Tom hasn't had time to put his clothes in the closet.	☐	☐
6 At the moment, Tom doesn't mind not having a freezer.	☐	☐
7 Tom would prefer different wallpaper in his new home.	☐	☐
8 Tom is confident that Sam will really like his apartment.	☐	☐

READING

1 Read the blog about house-sharing. Check (✓) the correct sentences, according to the information in the blog.

1. Real estate prices are rising, so more people share houses today than ever before. ____
2. People often need to share houses or apartments, but there can be problems. ____
3. You need to make sure your new roommate can afford to live there. ____
4. Feelings are important, but you can take practical steps to make sharing a house or apartment successful. ____
5. If you can't share with someone you know, you should at least meet the person before you move in together. ____
6. You should make a list of important things about where you are going to live. ____

2 Are the sentences true (T), false (F), or isn't there enough information to decide (N)?

1. Many people have bad experiences with roommates. ____
2. Mollie's roommate didn't know how to use their washing machine. ____
3. Jamie liked his roommate's snake. ____
4. A lot of people move into houses or apartments they can't really afford. ____
5. Becky's roommate was often late paying her rent. ____
6. It doesn't matter why someone left the last place they lived. ____
7. Daniel didn't like the type of music his roommates played. ____
8. If you don't feel comfortable with someone, you should find out where they lived before. ____
9. Websites can be a good place to find house-sharing opportunities. ____
10. At a speed housemating event, you can immediately find out basic information about people. ____

HOME BLOG PODCASTS ABOUT CONTACT

Guest blogger Penny explains how to find the perfect housemate.

The highs and lows of house-sharing

You want to leave home, but you can't afford your own apartment or house. What do you do? Sharing accommodations with other people in the same situation is the obvious answer. But how do you find those people, and how do you know you will get along with them? The Internet is full of horror stories, and here are a few of them!

"One of my roommates never changed his sheets," says 21-year-old Mollie Goodman. "Eventually the whole house started to smell!" 23-year-old Jamie King also had bad experiences. "In one place I lived, this guy moved in and brought a huge snake with him. Even worse, he filled the freezer with dead mice to feed it!"

Of course, money's another issue. You might be embarrassed to ask someone how they plan to pay the rent, but you don't want to end up like Becky. Her roommate claimed to be an actor, but the truth was that she was usually out of work. Not only did she rarely pay her rent on time, she also thought it was OK to use Becky's shampoo, drink her milk, and even "borrow" her clothes (without asking, of course!).

If you're the person moving into a house or apartment, find out why the last person left. Maybe, like Daniel Mills, 24, it was because the others were all in a band together, and rehearsed at home! I never got a moment's peace; it was terrible!" he says. If you're the one with a spare room, always ask for references from the people they lived with before. And listen to your heart. If you have a bad feeling about someone, just walk away. But listen to your head as well. Even if someone seems great, get an agreement in writing.

Most of us would prefer to live with someone we know, but that's not always possible, especially when you move to a new city. Online house-sharing sites are a good place to start. But one thing everyone agrees on is that you must meet the people you're going to live with face to face before you move in. Because this can take a lot of time, "speed housemating" events are becoming more and more popular. At these events people with rooms can meet people who want to rent. Everyone wears a sticker showing their budget and where they want to live. It's like speed dating, but with a front door key thrown in!

UNIT 12

People and relationships

12A LANGUAGE

GRAMMAR: Restrictive relative clauses

1 Choose the correct options to complete the sentences.

1 Did you see the photo *who / that or - / where* I posted yesterday?
2 Is that the neighbor *who / which / where* made the cake for your birthday?
3 That building on the left is the office *which / who / where* I used to work.
4 The woman *where / who / which* usually cuts my hair has left.
5 He loves playing sports *where / that or - / who* he hasn't tried before.
6 She told me about a restaurant *that / where / which* they make really good vegetarian food.
7 We could meet at that French café–the one *that or - / where / who* you mentioned earlier.
8 For people *which / who / where* prefer peace and quiet, this hotel is perfect.
9 Is she the girl *that or - / where / which* you were telling me about?
10 This is the room *that / which / where* most of the meetings take place.

2 Combine the two sentences using a relative pronoun.

1 That's the hotel. We stayed there in May.
______________________.
2 I lost the necklace. Marta gave it to me for my birthday.
______________________.
3 Did you hear the joke? Alan told it earlier.
______________________.
4 She shouted to the boy. He had dropped his phone.
______________________.
5 This is the bus. It goes to Chicago.
______________________.
6 Are they going to the restaurant? It opened last month.
______________________.

VOCABULARY: Relationships

3 Order the letters to make words that match the definitions.

1 someone who you share a house or apartment with OOMRETAM ______________
2 a person or organization that gives people work REPLOYME ______________
3 someone who hates another person and tries to harm them MEENY ______________
4 someone that you work with GLOECLEAU ______________
5 someone that you live near to HENIGROB ______________
6 a man who is getting married or has just got married MOROG ______________
7 someone who you own a company with SUBISSEN TRAPERN ______________
8 the brother of your husband or wife, or your sister's husband ROBERTH-NI-WAL ______________

4 Complete the words. Some letters are given.

1 My father left when we were little, so my mother was a s___ ___ ___ ___ ___ parent.
2 My mother remarried and had a daughter, so I have a s___ ___ ___ ___ ___ ___ ___ ___ ___ ___.
3 She has one cousin living near her, but no other r___ ___ ___ ___ ___ ___ ___ ___ .
4 I don't have brothers or sisters; I'm an o___ ___ ___ child.
5 Sarah doesn't get along with her husband's parents, but I love my i___ -l___ ___s.
6 My aunts and uncles all have children, so I have lots of c___ ___ ___ ___ ___ ___ ___.
7 I didn't like the last guy I worked for, but my new b___ ___ ___ is great.
8 Ted's g___ ___ ___ ___ ___ ___ ___ ___ ___ ___ came to the nightclub; they've been going out for six months.

PRONUNCIATION: Sentence stress

5 ▶ 12.1 Look at the relative pronouns *who, which,* and *where*. Are they stressed (S) or unstressed (U)? Listen, check, and repeat.

1 Who did you speak to? **S U**
2 That's the town where he grew up. **S U**
3 She must be the woman who works here. **S U**
4 Where are the instructions? **S U**
5 Did she say which flight she was taking? **S U**
6 Which jacket looks better with these pants? **S U**

READING: Interpreting data

A

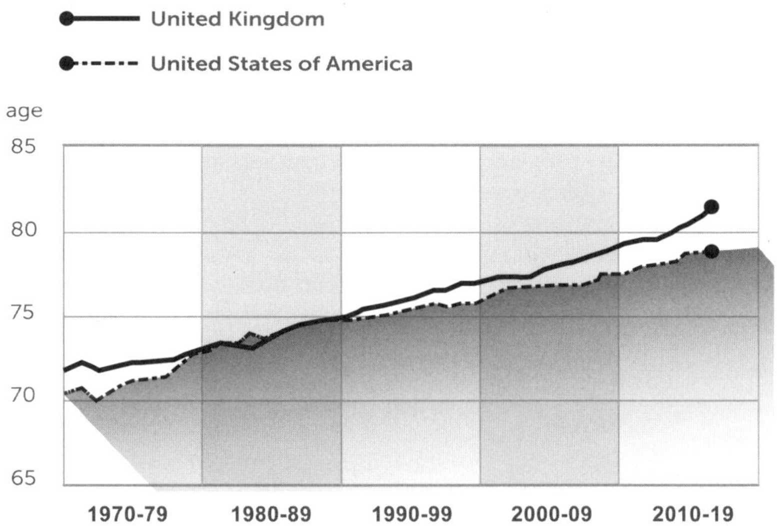

B

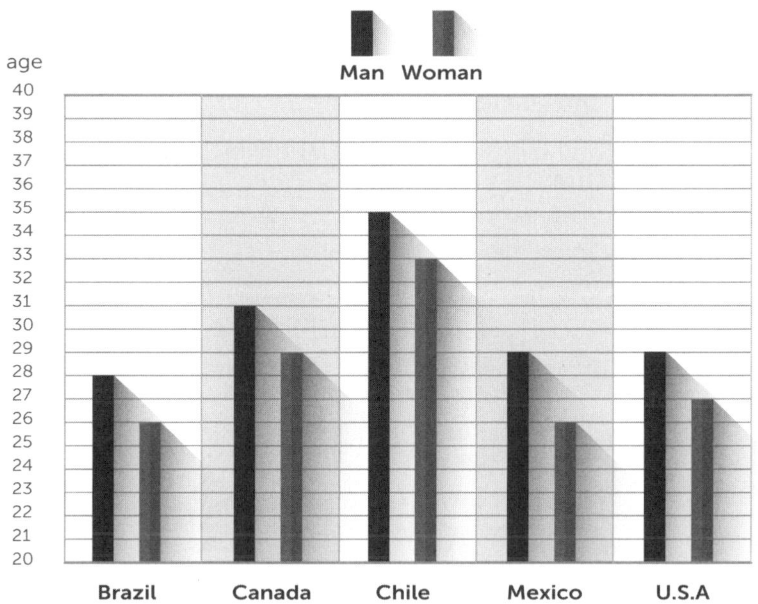

C

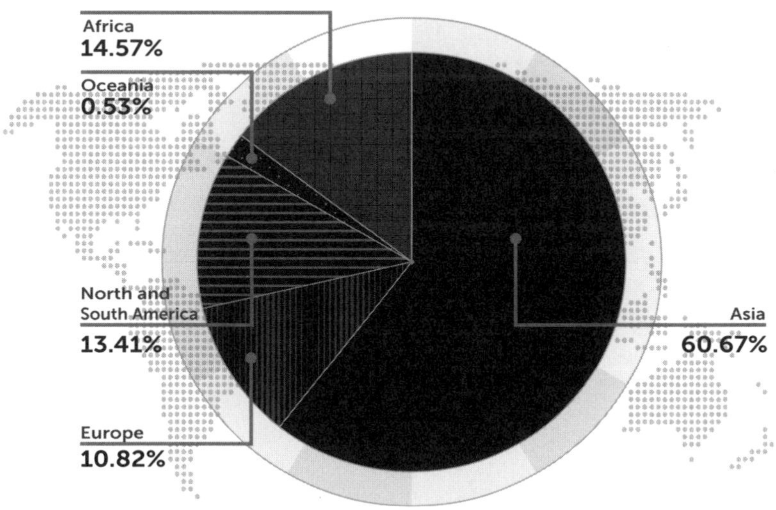

1 Match the information in Graphs A–C with three of 1–6.

1 World population by continent. ____
2 Average temperatures by continent. ____
3 Male and female life expectancy. ____
4 Average age of first marriage. ____
5 U.K. and U.S. population change. ____
6 Life expectancy in the U.S. and U.K. ____

2 According to Graphs A–C, are these statements true (T) or false (F)?

1 Life expectancy in the U.S. rose by more than five years from 1990 to 2010. ____
2 In 1980, life expectancy for both U.K. and U.S. citizens was still less than 75. ____
3 The difference between life expectancy in the U.K. and the U.S. increased from 1990 to 2010. ____
4 The average age difference between men and women for their first marriage is two years everywhere except Canada. ____
5 Chilean people are older at the time of their first marriage than other nationalities on this chart. ____
6 Brazilian women are the same age as women from the U.S. when they get married for the first time. ____
7 Asia has the highest population of any continent. ____
8 The population of Africa is about 3% larger than that of North and South America. ____
9 Fewer people live in North and South America than in Europe. ____

3 Choose the correct options to complete this summary of Graph A.

Graph A shows that from 1970 to 2012, U.K. citizens almost always lived slightly [1]*longer / shorter* lives than U.S. citizens. Both groups have [2]*increased / decreased* their life expectancy by [3]*around / at least* 10 years during the period shown. From 1970 to 1979, life expectancy for U.S. citizens increased by [4]*at least / nearly* five years. From 1975 to 1995, data for the U.K. and the U.S. were [5]*not at all / roughly* similar. However, for a brief time around 1980, the life expectancy of U.S. citizens was just [6]*over / under* that of people in the U.K. By 1982, life expectancy in both the U.S. and the U.K. had reached [7]*at least / almost* 75. By 2012, the average person in the U.K. could expect to live to [8]*at least / nearly* 80.

GRAMMAR: Uses of the *-ing* form and the infinitive

1 Choose the correct options to complete the sentences.

1 I was disappointed about ____ the exam.
a to fail b failing
2 Before ____ , maybe we should have something to eat.
a to leave b leaving
3 She just left the office ____ some lunch.
a getting b to get
4 ____ is the best form of exercise.
a To walk b Walking
5 I agree there's a problem, although I think it's unfair ____ Jim.
a blaming b to blame
6 It's not expensive ____ on a camping trip.
a going b to go
7 It was impossible not ____ her my secret!
a to tell b telling
8 ____ time with friends is so important.
a Spending b To spend
9 Not ____ meat can be difficult in some countries.
a to eat b eating

2 Complete the sentences with the verbs in the box. Use each verb twice, once in the *-ing* form and once in the infinitive.

earn see discuss eat speak

1 She was too afraid ____________ to her boss about the situation.
2 We were both hungry, so we went home ____________.
3 ____________ a lot of money is hard work.
4 After ____________ the matter, we came to a decision.
5 Are you interested in ____________ a movie this evening?
6 ____________ to a room of two hundred people is terrifying.
7 I'd be interested ____________ her face when she hears the news!
8 I was delighted ____________ a little extra money.
9 Fernando and I met ____________ the problem.
10 ____________ a lot of sugar is bad for your health.

VOCABULARY: Relationship verbs

3 Choose the correct options to complete the sentences.

1 I met a really nice girl on Saturday and thought I might ____ her **out**.
a keep b ask c go
2 Karla and Javier ended their relationship, but ____ **back together** last month.
a got b fell c broke
3 Did you know that Bernie and Karen are ____ **married** next year?
a making b getting c going
4 Joe and Eve used to go ____ **together**, but they broke up.
a on b in c out
5 Connie is **going on** a ____ tonight with a guy she met at work.
a date b marriage c break
6 I've known Pablo for ten years. We ____ **friends** when we lived in Mexico City.
a became b got c went

4 Complete the sentences.

1 Although Laura and I ive in different countries, we manage to stay in ____________.
2 They met and ____________ in love while they were in college.
3 We have similar interests and opinions. In general, we ____________ a lot in common.
4 Nancy is single again. She broke ____________ with her boyfriend a week ago.
5 Alejandro seems interesting. I'd like to ____________ to know him better.
6 Isabella's great! I've always gotten ____________ really well with her.

PRONUNCIATION: Word stress

5 12.2 Match 1–8 with stress patterns a–e. Listen, check and repeat.

1 important ____
2 colleague ____
3 impossible ____
4 except ____
5 technology ____
6 better ____
7 afraid ____
8 probably ____

a O o
b o O
c o O o
d O o o
e o O o o

SPEAKING: Saying thanks

1 ▶ 12.3 Listen to the conversation between Anna and Tim. Which four of these phrases do they use? Number them 1–4 in the order that you hear them.

- **a** Thanks a lot. ____
- **b** That's very nice of you. ____
- **c** Thanks a million. ____
- **d** Thanks. ____
- **e** Thank you so much. ____
- **f** Thanks very much. ____
- **g** I can't thank you enough. ____
- **h** I really appreciate it. ____
- **i** I'm very grateful to you. ____

2 Read the four phrases from the conversation. Match them to the different ways of responding modestly.

1. Oh, I'm glad you like it. It's a really easy recipe. ____ ____
2. Not at all. It would be a lot of fun. ____
3. It's nothing, really! ____
4. Well, to be honest, not many other people entered. ____

- **a** saying you are pleased
- **b** saying something isn't difficult
- **c** saying something is not as good as the other person thinks
- **d** saying you would enjoy doing something
- **e** saying something is only a small thing

3 ▶ 12.4 Listen to five people speaking. Choose the most appropriate response.

1. *That's very nice of you. / Thanks.*
2. *Thanks a lot. / I'm very grateful to you.*
3. *Thanks very much. / I really appreciate it.*
4. *Thanks a lot. / I can't thank you enough.*
5. *I can't thank you enough. / Thanks a million.*

4 ▶ 12.5 Listen to four people thanking, congratulating or complimenting you. Use your own ideas to respond modestly.

1. You're welcome. ____________________.
2. I'm glad you think so, but ____________________.
3. No problem. ____________________
4. Thanks. ____________________

5 ▶ 12.6 Listen to some possible answers to exercise 4.

HOME BLOG PODCASTS ABOUT CONTACT

Tom and Sam talk about friendship and romance.

LISTENING

1 12.7 Listen to the podcast. Are the statements true (T) or false (F), according to the speaker?

1 Sophie didn't get along with Marco to begin with. ____
2 Friendships can become romantic relationships. ____
3 What makes a good friend also makes a good partner. ____

2 12.7 Listen again. Choose the correct options to complete the sentences.

1 Sophie met Marco in
  a school.
  b college.
  c work.
2 When they were in college, they
  a rarely spoke to each other.
  b never spoke to each other.
  c were in contact with each other.
3 In New York, Sophie and Marco fell in love
  a over a period of time.
  b immediately.
  c with other people.
4 Sophie says that when two people start going out together, they
  a can be too honest with each other.
  b usually feel better about themselves.
  c often try to appear better than they are.
5 When Sophie started going out with Marco, she
  a already knew his personality.
  b didn't really like it.
  c found out new things about him.
6 Sophie says that people often choose a partner because
  a they have lots in common.
  b of their appearance.
  c of their honesty.
7 She says that finding someone physically attractive
  a may not be enough in a relationship.
  b is often bad for a relationship.
  c is usually good for a relationship.

READING

1 Read the blog about five people's problems. Complete 1–5 with the words in the box. There are three extra words.

classmate	partners	boss	roommate
neighbors	colleagues	relative	girlfriend

2 Match the advice in 1–8 with problems A–E.

1 You should try to get to know the people you work with. ____
2 It's not a good idea to communicate with this person. ____
3 You might meet someone special through your friends. ____
4 You have to remember that most people are busy. ____
5 There's not much you can do to change this situation. ____
6 Think of ways to start up a conversation with them. ____
7 Most people experience this at some point in their life. ____
8 You're unlikely to make friends at work if you're the boss. ____

HOME BLOG PODCASTS ABOUT CONTACT

Tom and Sam give some advice about readers' problems.

You have your say

We've learned so much about other people through writing this blog. Since this is our last one, we've invited our readers to write in with their problems to see if we can give them some advice.

A *We've just moved to a new town. No one talks to us or shows any interest, and we feel we're not welcome. Can you help?*

It's not that your [1]__________ dislike you–they're just going on with their lives, going to work, seeing their friends, etc., and that doesn't leave much time for you! Why not invent a reason to talk to them? Ask when the next garbage pick-up is, or which items you can recycle. People generally like to be helpful and the conversation might lead to other things.

B *I have a small company and my employees get along well. The problem is that they treat me differently. They never talk to me during their breaks or ask me to go out with them.*

To be honest, you probably just have to accept it. Your employees may respect you, even like you, but you're not their friend–you're their [2]__________ and you have a different relationship with them. If you're short of friends, you need to look in other places.

C *I broke up with my [3]__________ last week and it's all I can think about. I'm OK at work, but at home I don't know what to do with myself. I feel so sad and lonely.*

You probably won't like this, but you have to stop thinking about her. The relationship's over—she's made that clear. Get out and meet new people and you'll stop thinking about her.

D *I'm a single parent. I have great friends, but they're all getting married or have girlfriends or boyfriends, and I'm always the lonely guy at the party. Any ideas?*

So your friends all have [4]__________. It happens to everyone after a certain age. But why aren't they introducing you to their single friends? Why not suggest it? After all, if you get along with them, there's a good chance you'll get along with their friends. One of them may be your future partner!

E *I moved here recently for a new job, and I don't know anyone. I'm single, and I'm spending all my time alone. I'd love to make friends, but I'm shy.*

Come on, don't wait for people to come to you! What about those new [5]__________? Use your coffee breaks to get to know them. You'll soon find you have things in common and the next thing you know, you'll be watching movies together!

WRITING: Making notes

1 Read Anup's blog about the best year of his life. Then complete it with reasons and results a–f.

a it had been snowing heavily
b I started talking to a young woman on the platform
c I was able to travel and see the world
d it reminds me of that wonderful year
e I really wanted to go there
f it was so interesting

This photograph shows me in front of the Taj Mahal in India. The year was 2012, and it was the best year of my life!

I finished college that summer, but my new job didn't start until the end of the year. That's why [1]________________. I spent a lot of that time in India, and it was absolutely amazing! I went to England as a young child, but I was born in India, so [2]________________. I even brought back some photos of the house where I'd lived with my parents.

In November of that year, I finally started my career as a journalist. It was hard work, but that's why [3]________________. I was lucky to have a fantastic boss who taught me a lot, and it was great to have a job that I knew I was going to love.

And finally, the best thing of all that happened in 2012, was that one day my train was two hours late because [4]________________. I was bored and fed up, so [5]________________. Did I fall in love that day? Well, maybe not that day, but I did like her enough to invite her to dinner, and we got married two years later.

Life is still great, but if I need to cheer myself up for any reason, I get this photo out and look at it because [6]________________.

2 Think about the best year of your life. Write notes about it on the mind map. You can invent ideas—they don't have to be true! You can leave some clouds empty or add new clouds.

3 Read the sentences. Do they talk about reasons or results?

1 2014 was the best year of my life because I got my driver's license that year. reason result
2 I wanted to be a doctor, so I had to work hard in school. reason result
3 I went swimming every day. That's why I was in such good shape. reason result
4 My boss was out of town, so I had the chance to do her job. reason result
5 I was really pleased because I passed all my exams. reason result

4 Write three sentences like the ones in exercise 3. Use *because, so,* and *That's why* and ideas from your mind map.

5 Write a blog about the best year of your life.

- Write about at least three good things that happened, using your notes from exercise 2.
- Write as many ideas as you can about these three main topics.
- Choose the best ideas then organize them into three paragraphs.
- Include at least three sentences with *because, so,* or *that's why.*

WRITING: Writing a narrative

1 Read the story about how Ed got a job. Which paragraph (1–4) is missing?

1 the background 2 a problem 3 a resolution 4 the ending

It was 2014, and I wasn't happy. There I was, 22 years old, with a good degree in computer studies, but I was working as a waiter for a company that didn't treat its employees well. I kept applying for computer jobs, but companies always wanted people with experience working with computers. Without a job, I couldn't get experience, and without experience, I couldn't get a job. The situation seemed impossible.

Then one day, I was working at a party given by a large car company. Before the guests started eating, the boss wanted to give a presentation. He was using notes that were on his computer, but in the middle of his presentation, it suddenly stopped working.

He tried hard to fix the problem, but it still wouldn't work. He started to look nervous. Everyone was waiting for him to finish speaking so they could eat. When I offered to help, he looked surprised, but agreed to let me try. Fortunately, I immediately saw what was wrong and quickly got his computer working again.

2 Complete the sentences with the simple past or past continuous form of the verbs in parentheses..

1 Ed was working as a waiter, but he ______ for a better job at the same time. (look)
2 Ed ______ to be a waiter. (not want)
3 Ed ______ enough experience to get a computer job. (not have)
4 The boss's computer stopped working while he ______. (speak)
5 Ed successfully ______ the computer. (fix)

3 Find words in the story to complete these sentences. Are they adjectives or adverbs?

1 Ed didn't feel ______ in 2014. adjective adverb
2 The waiters weren't treated ______. adjective adverb
3 The computer ______ stopped working. adjective adverb
4 The boss tried ______ to get the the computer to work again. adjective adverb
5 He began to look ______. adjective adverb
6 Ed repaired the computer ______. adjective adverb

4 Use these pictures to write the missing paragraph of the story.

- Try to write five sentences. Describe what happened, how Ed felt, and what the situation is now.
- Use verbs in the simple past and past continuous.
- Use adjectives and adverbs to make your paragraph interesting.

WRITING: Writing an informal e-mail asking for advice

1 Read Michael's e-mail asking for advice about a trip. Then number a–i in the order in which they appear in the e-mail (1–9). The first answer is given.

To: robknight5@openmail.com

RE: Advice

Hi Rob!

[1]How's it going? Are you still going running every day? [2]I'm going climbing in the Himalayas in the spring, but I'm a little worried about it. That's why I'm writing. I know [3]you've been to Nepal, and I wanted to ask you for some advice.

I really love walking, as you know, but I've never done anything like this. It sounds extremely tough and I'm scared [4]it'll be too difficult for me. I'm not in very good shape right now. What do you think I should do? Can you give me some ideas about how to prepare, and what I should take with me? [5]What's the best way to get in better shape in three months?? Can you send me some tips?

Anyway, I guess [6]it's good to try new things. Seb told me you've taken up painting. He says [7]you're pretty good at it!

Do you feel like going for coffee sometime soon? Then I can ask you some more questions about my trip.

See you later,

Michael

- **a** asking about the person you're writing to ____
- **b** the ending ____
- **c** the greeting ____
- **d** making an arrangement ____
- **e** the reason for writing ____
- **f** the request for a response ____
- **g** mentioning a different subject ____
- **h** the subject _1_
- **i** the details of the problem ____

2 Look at the underlined contractions in the e-mail (1–7) and write the full forms.

3 Complete these phrases from the e-mail with modifiers. Then number them 1–5, from the strongest to the weakest.

1 I'm ____________ worried about it. ____
2 I ____________ love walking, as you know ... ____
3 It sounds ____________ tough ... ____
4 I'm not in ____________ good shape right now. ____
5 ... he says you're ____________ good at it! ____

4 Read the problem in the box, then write an e-mail to a friend, asking for advice.

> You have decided to take up a sport or activity that involves a risk.
> Your parents think it is too dangerous and they don't want you to do it.
> You want to do it, but you don't want to hurt yourself.

- Structure the e-mail with a subject, greeting, reason for writing, details, request for response, and an ending.
- Use contractions like *I'm* and *don't*.
- Use informal words and phrases like *Hi, How's it going?*, and *anyway*.
- Use modifiers like *extremely* and *a little* to make adjectives and adverbs stronger or weaker.

WRITING: Writing an essay

1 Read the essay about eating meat and put paragraphs A–E in order. Use the linkers to help you (*First, The second reason, Finally, In conclusion*).

A ____ **B** ____ **C** ____ **D** ____ **E** ____

Should humans stop eating meat?

A The second reason is the environment. Raising animals for food produces gases that increase global warming. In addition, the animals need to be given huge amounts of water and grain. Also, some studies say that we would need twenty times less land to feed people instead of animals.

B People have been eating meat for thousands of years, and they seem to love it. According to one report, the average American eats around 25 kilos of beef, 27 kilos of chicken and 22 kilos of pork in a year. But is it a good idea to go on like this? I don't believe that it is.

C In conclusion, I realize that many people love eating meat, but I would say that vegetarian food can be just as tasty. In any case, our world is changing. We are facing serious problems of climate change, obesity, and disease, and, in my opinion, it's time for us to change too—before it's too late.

D First, there's the question of the animals themselves. We go to a supermarket and buy a piece of meat in a package, but that meat was once a little lamb or a cute calf. Personally, I love all animals and I don't want to eat them!

E Finally, there is more and more evidence that eating fruit and vegetables is healthy and eating too much meat is not. I'm worried that diseases such as diabetes and heart disease are becoming more common because many people eat too much, and in particular too much meat.

2 The author talks about three main issues: protecting animals (A), the environment (E), and our health (H). Write the correct letter next to the arguments she uses.

1 There would be more food for people if we didn't eat meat. ____
2 A vegetarian diet is better for people than eating meat. ____
3 We don't think about animals enough when we eat them. ____
4 Eating meat may be increasing diseases. ____
5 The gas from keeping animals leads to global warming. ____
6 Obesity is a serious problem. ____

3 Read the opinions about "meat-free Monday"–the idea that you should have one day a week without meat. Complete them with the words in the box, then say if each one is for (F) or against (A) meat-free Monday.

think delighted worried say bad opinion personally good

1 In my ____________, we need meat to stay strong and healthy.
2 ____________, I feel much healthier when I don't eat meat.
3 It's always a ____________ idea to eat more vegetables.
4 I ____________ our bodies and teeth are designed to eat meat.
5 I'm ____________ farmers would suffer.
6 I would ____________ that vegetarian food can be as tasty as meat.
7 I'm ____________ more people are giving up meat because I love animals.
8 It's a ____________ idea to stop eating meat because it makes us stronger.

4 Write an essay on the subject "Everyone should have a meat-free Monday."

- You can use ideas from exercise 3 or your own ideas.
- Organize your ideas into five paragraphs: introduction, reasons 1–3, conclusion.
- Give examples and evidence to support your reasons.
- Use the linkers from exercise 1.

WRITING: Writing a formal e-mail

1 Read Ben's formal e-mail complaining about his gym classes. What is the correct order of the paragraphs?

1 ____ 2 ____ 3 ____

To: info@gymsforall.com

Subject: Exercise classes

[1]*Dear Sir/Madam:*

A

In recent weeks, a large number of classes [2]*have been canceled* without notice. [3]*In addition to this,* several of the teachers appear to be extremely inexperienced, leading to a real risk of injury.

B

In my opinion, all exercise instructors should [4]*be checked* regularly to [5]*ensure* that [6]*they are* teaching to the highest standards. Would you please let me know as soon as possible how you intend to improve this unsatisfactory situation.

C

[7]*I am writing* [8]*with regard to* the standard of the exercise classes at your gym, which I believe has reached an [9]*unacceptable* level.

[10]*Regards,*

Ben Southgate

2 Look at words and phrases 1–10 in the e-mail and write the numbers next to the correct feature of formal e-mails.

Formal greeting	____
Using full forms, not contractions	____ ____
Formal words and expressions	____ ____ ____ ____
Passives to avoid being personal	____ ____
Formal ending	____

3 Order the letters to form nouns to complete the sentences. What is the verb form of each noun?

1 The dressing rooms need a lot of i____________. NTPRMOEVME
2 Gym members need better instructions to avoid i____________. RUJNY
3 Prices are already high. An i____________ is unreasonable. RENCASE
4 Changes to class schedules have caused c____________. NFUONOSI
5 The m____________ should run the gym more efficiently. NTNAGAEME
6 We are not given enough i____________ about how to use the equipment safely. NFROAMITNO
7 The d____________ that we were being given dirty towels was shocking. COVISERY
8 I have made the d____________ to cancel my membership. ISCENOI
9 Your plan to raise the price came as an unwelcome s____________. REURPSI

4 You have received an e-mail telling you that the cost of your gym membership is going up. You feel this is unreasonable because of the poor quality of the gym. Write a formal e-mail of complaint.

- Include three paragraphs: say why you are writing, explain the situation, and say what you want to be done.
- Use the features of formal e-mails in exercise 2.
- Use the sentences in exercise 3 for ideas.

WRITING: Making writing interesting

1 Read Eva's description of her first meeting with her neighbor. Choose the correct words to complete the text.

The first time I met Davina, I was very scared of her! It was only the second day in my apartment when she knocked on my door to complain that I was being too noisy. [1]*However / As well / Although* it was two o'clock in the afternoon, she was wearing a pair of pajamas with a huge old black coat on top. Her long blonde hair was sticking up all over the place. She looked really sleepy, and really angry, [2]*too / also / however*.

She told me she was a nurse and she was trying to sleep [3]*because / so / that's why* she had been working all night. [4]*But / That's why / And* she was wearing pajamas. Of course, I apologized. I suddenly realized how loud my music was [5]*because / too / so* I wasn't surprised she was annoyed.

I felt really bad. [6]*Although / That's why / However*, the next day a card was slid under my door, inviting me for coffee on the weekend. That's when I discovered that Davina is really a lovely person when she's not tired!

Now we get along really well. We sometimes go out together, and I [7]*also / as well / too* take care of her friendly little brown and white cat when she goes out of town. Of course, I'm not frightened of her any more, [8]*but / because / also* I never play loud music now!

2 Look at the underlined words in Eva's description and make four pairs of synonyms.

3 Look at the adjectives in these sentences. Write them in the correct columns.

1. My roommate is a **lovely young Italian** woman.
2. We sat at a **big round wood** table.
3. Milo had **beautiful long brown** hair.
4. Hannah was wearing a **blue cotton** shirt.
5. Chris has a **fat old black** dog.
6. Karl cooks **delicious French** food.

opinion	size	shape	age	colour	nationality	material

4 Write about the first time you met someone you have a relationship with now, for example, a neighbor, friend, colleague, or roommate.

- Use interesting adjectives, in the correct order, to describe things.
- Use synonyms to avoid repeating words.
- Use linkers to give reasons and results (*so, because, that's why*), to contrast information (*but, although, however*) or add information (*and, also, too, as well*).

Richmond
58 St Aldates
Oxford
OX1 1ST
United Kingdom

Printed in Mexico
ISBN: 978-84-668-2889-5
CP: 641995

Publishing Director: Deborah Tricker
Publisher: Luke Baxter
Editor: Helen Wendholt
Proofreaders: Tas Cooper, Fiona Hunt, Amanda Leigh
Design Manager: Lorna Heaslip
Cover Design: Richmond
Design & Layout: Lorna Heaslip, Oliver Hutton, Gabriela Álvarez
Photo Researcher: Magdalena Mayo
Audio production: TEFL Audio
Americanization: Diane Hermanson

Illustrators:
Liav Zabari, c/o Lemonade Illustration Agency

Photos:
ALAMY/Frances Roberts, Nick Baylis, REUTERS, David Taylor, Paul Nichols, Mode Images, M L Pearson, Jeremey Richards, Panther Media GmBH, Big Cheese Photo LLC, Digital Image Library, Sabena Jane Blackbird, www.BibleLandPictures.com, Purcell Team; GETTY IMAGES SALES SPAIN/Thinkstock; ISTOCKPHOTO/Getty Images Sales Spain; REX SHUTTERSTOCK/Solent News; ARCHIVO SANTILLANA

Cover Photo: Jon Barlow

We would like to thank the following reviewers for their valuable feedback which has made Personal Best possible. We extend our thanks to the many teachers and students not mentioned here.
Brad Bawtinheimer, Manuel Hidalgo, Paulo Dantas, Diana Bermúdez, Laura Gutiérrez, Hardy Griffin, Angi Conti, Christopher Morabito, Hande Kokce, Jorge Lobato, Leonardo Mercato, Mercilinda Ortiz, Wendy López

The Publisher has made every effort to trace the owner of copyright material; however, the Publisher will correct any involuntary omission at the earliest opportunity.

Printed in Mexico by Corporativo Prográfico, S.A. de C.V., Calle Dos Núm. 257, Bodega 4, Col. Granjas San Antonio, C.P.09070, Del. Iztapalapa, México, Ciudad de México, in july 2017.